The Gifted Parenting Journey

A Guide to Self-Discovery and Support
for Families of Gifted Children

Gail Post, Ph.D.

D1607440

Gifted
UNLIMITED

Edited by: Ramona DuBose, Molly A. Isaacs-McLeod
Interior design: The Printed Page
Cover design: Kelly Crimi

Published by
Gifted Unlimited, LLC
12340 U.S. Highway 42, No. 453
Goshen, KY 40026
www.giftedunlimitedllc.com

© 2022 by Gail Post

ISBN: 978-1-953360-15-1

Dedication

Writing may be an isolating activity, but creating a book is an act of collaboration. My inspiration for this project was sparked by countless interactions with parents of the gifted who readily shared their stories. Each parent, each client, each friend, each colleague experienced their own unique journey, yet all shared similar emotions. Isolation. Exuberance. Uncertainty. Exasperation. Joy. And an overriding sense of wonder.

I, too, was schooled through an immersion in the gifted parenting experience and from daily interactions with my children, teachers, colleagues, friends, and clients. I am ever grateful for the support and encouragement found through conversations with fellow parents— bonds forged through camaraderie and commiseration following school board meetings, in hallways outside of chess tournaments, during concert intermissions, and in homes where plans for challenging school policy were fomented. I remain in awe of the wise, caring, and accessible teachers who provided guidance to my children and who demonstrated how gifted education could and should be provided, despite the systemic roadblocks that impeded their efforts. My learning curve was fueled by the many articles and books I consumed; I have enormous appreciation for my colleagues, many of whom are talented writers, and for those leaders in the gifted field whom I have not met, but whose research, publications, and advocacy served as inspiration.

I am honored that so many families have entrusted me with their emotions, graciously shared during psychotherapy, at parenting workshops, or in response to my blog posts and articles. Their quandaries and struggles—ubiquitous among most parents of the gifted—served as a catalyst for writing this book. "The Gifted Parenting Journey" was grounded in the recognition that self-awareness and support are key to better parenting. Little had been written about what parents of the gifted think and feel; my hope was that this book would fill a gap within the gifted literature. Writing is a personal joy for me; it has been a privilege to use this medium to highlight the gifted parenting experience. I am also thankful for my early training as a musician, and appreciate how much the interplay of rhythm and intonation found in music has influenced my writing process.

I am immensely grateful to my publisher, Molly Isaacs-McLeod, who enthusiastically embraced the concept for the book and always remained cheerful, supportive, and open to granting me the freedom I craved, without constraints. Many thanks go out to her support staff on the Gifted Unlimited team who helped this book come to life. I am indebted to the many parents who participated in the gifted parenting survey that I launched while writing this book. Their moving accounts of raising gifted children, expressed in hundreds of raw, personal, heartfelt comments that accompanied the survey responses, were so very much appreciated.

On a more personal note, I am deeply grateful to those closest to me. My wonderful and amazing friends generously offered their overwhelming enthusiasm throughout this writing journey—their kindness both humbles and astonishes me. My husband, Frank, endured my frustrations, uncertainty, and excitement as this project unfolded, yet offered his unwavering support. But most of all, I am endlessly grateful for the gift of experiencing life with my two sons, Matthew and Daniel. In many ways, they taught me everything I needed to know.

Contents

Introduction

Surprise! Your child is gifted!

You may have recently discovered that your child is gifted—and you're trembling in your boots. Excited, yes. But, also keenly aware that nurturing your child's abilities requires a different trajectory than what you might expect if you were raising a neurotypical child. You didn't bargain for this. You didn't ask for it. Yet here you are—facing an exciting, challenging, and at times, daunting journey ahead.

Perhaps your child's giftedness wasn't such a surprise. Maybe you suspected it when they spoke in full sentences as a toddler. Perhaps their curiosity about the meaning of life was both startling and profound. Maybe your child's artistic or spatial or mathematical skills are astonishing. Perhaps you hail from a long line of gifted folks in your family—and if you admitted it to yourself, you might acknowledge that you are gifted as well.

Prepared or not, you face a unique parenting journey—one that differs from what many other parents experience. It is likely that you will feel exhilarating pride, worry about your child's quirks and social mishaps, and endure frustrating roadblocks in your attempts to ensure an education your child deserves. And since giftedness—typically identified by an IQ score of 130 or higher—comprises roughly 1-5% of the population, you rarely cross paths with other parents of gifted children. This can leave you feeling isolated and misunderstood.

What is so challenging about parenting a gifted child?

Gifted abilities are viewed by many as a ticket to the good life. There is a widespread notion that the gifted are privileged. They are often viewed as downright lucky to possess the smarts, talent, and innate potential that should propel them toward future success. Who *wouldn't* want their child to be gifted?

It is not always that easy, though. Along with their keen intellect, gifted children can be a whirlwind of energy, emotionally intense, and an endless source of questions, questions, questions! You might find yourself disengaged from neighbors and family, as you feel compelled to apologize, explain, or clarify your child's offbeat behavior. You sometimes endure sleepless nights worrying about whether your child will fit in with peers or feel heartbreak over every social rejection. And you find yourself on a never-ending quest to secure an education that will meet your child's learning needs.

Nevertheless, many downplay and even scoff at these challenges. After all, why would a child with an exceptional IQ, amazing talents, and tremendous potential need additional support? Don't these fortunate children just cruise through school, waltz into an ivy league college, and then land a cushy job on Wall Street? They are blessed with the "gift" of intelligence and talent, so what more do they need?

These common assumptions pervade society's impressions of the gifted. Often fueled by negative stereotypes in media and film, along with a dearth of clear information, those who are uninformed sometimes dismiss or even disparage the social, emotional, and academic needs of the gifted. And this can be damaging. The uninformed exist among those who influence school policy. They teach your children. They hint to their kids that your child is just a little too weird. They lob snide comments across the table at family gatherings. Their actions can instill feelings of shame, inadequacy, and hopelessness in the children we love.

The gifted are mocked in film and the media, portrayed as nerds, losers, inept geniuses, arrogant jerks, and social misfits. The proverbial

"Sheldons" and "Sherlocks" inhabit a skewed and one-dimensional stereotype. Men are often portrayed as effeminate and women as unattractive. For every talent and gift, there is a flaw set in place to counterbalance and offset any threat that high intellect imposes. The pursuit of knowledge is sometimes viewed with suspicion. Presidents are chosen because they are "someone I'd like to have a beer with," and anti-intellectual sentiment is flourishing. Politics aside, there are widespread misconceptions about the gifted within every community, among every socioeconomic class, and across political party lines.

How does this affect your child?

What happens if you are a gifted child, growing up in a world filled with mixed messages? On the one hand, your accomplishments are praised, and sometimes parents or teachers seem amazed by what they deem an unusual feat. On the other, you quickly absorb messages from peers, the school culture, and the media about what is attractive and appealing. And you don't fit that mold. You might receive an award for your science fair project, but the "cool kid" who is funny and slacks off is much more popular. Perhaps you get teased for being a nerd or miss out on party invitations. Even some of your relatives make jokes about how brainy you are. Your basketball coach tells you to "stop hitting the books so much" and get out and play more. And your teacher seems frustrated with your probing questions and desire to learn. If you are "twice exceptional" (where you are intellectually gifted, but also struggle with additional challenges, such as a learning disability or attention deficit/hyperactivity disorder), you might feel even more misunderstood.

Eventually, you get the memo. You recognize that a lot of children—and adults—don't understand you. And many don't really like your abilities. They resent your talents, compete with you, and feel threatened. You realize that your teachers don't get it—or if they do understand, just don't have the time or energy to offer what you need. You might forge a perfectionistic path where you doggedly uphold the gifted persona others seem to expect—terrified of not being the best and disappointing yourself or others. Striving to be perfect is exhausting, especially when expectations are high and you already feel misunderstood. On the other hand, you might decide that accomplishments aren't worth it and coast through school without exerting any effort. You might even think that everything should be easy going forward, so you avoid classes or projects that seem difficult or do not guarantee success. You also realize that you have a choice; either embrace your "inner nerd" or hide your talents. If you want to be popular, you "dumb yourself down" so you can fit in.

Of course, denying your true nature is demoralizing. You start to feel bored, apathetic, and even hopeless. Learning used to be fun, but now it seems pointless. Sure, there may be a few topics that are engaging, and you might have some extracurricular activities that interest you, but the pace and depth of education is so slow that you lose all faith in the school. You might become what Delisle[1] labels a "selective consumer" and choose only those subjects that interest you. Or your underachievement goes unnoticed, given how effortlessly you acquire good grades, leaving you an "underachiever under-the-radar[2]." Since you never developed study skills, you are caught off-guard when you eventually encounter challenging classes. You even might drop out of school altogether. There are no good outcomes when you are never challenged in school.

And then, as a parent…

Many of you reading this will recognize your child's experience in the preceding paragraphs. While this trajectory does not apply to every gifted child, it characterizes the struggles gifted children routinely face. And, of course, it is even more alarming when it relates to *your* child. As a parent, you may be reeling from conformation that your child is gifted…or grappling with their uncanny smarts…or managing a whirlwind of energy and endless questioning. But the vast journey ahead looms with no clear roadmap and loads of unknowns. How do you ensure that school will be challenging? Will they find friends who "get them?" Can you afford after-school activities to support their interests? How do you explain to relatives that your child converses like an adult, but acts like a toddler when tired or upset? How do you protect them from perfectionism and anxiety and isolation and bullying and existential depression? *And how do you keep our own sanity as a parent—especially when others don't understand?*

Due to widespread misunderstanding and biases against gifted children, many parents feel almost as isolated as their kids. They often assume they must hide or downplay their child's accomplishments, may question whether their perceptions are accurate, and sometimes doubt their parenting abilities. Some worry whether they are, in fact, pushing their child too much, or conversely, not challenging them enough. They question how—and how much—to advocate in the schools, reluctant to be labeled "that pushy parent," the one who teachers avoid and disregard. They might even wonder if they are qualified to adequately raise and parent such a bright and talented person.

The good news is that *no one is better equipped to parent your child than you!* You know your child best, and possess the love, understanding, and dedication to offer everything they need. What *you* may need along the way, though, is support. Support to bolster your confidence, shore up your resolve, and keep you going on those rough days. Support to make hard choices, to push yourself beyond your limits (such as challenging so-called "authority" figures who misunderstand your child) or to view yourself differently (as you might discover that you are gifted, as well). Support to stand up to others. Support to guide your child through the long journey into adulthood. Support from other parents of gifted and high ability children who truly understand your experience.

How this book can guide you

Many excellent books about gifted children[3-9] offer guidelines for raising a gifted child. Most cover specific social, emotional, or academic challenges, with advice about addressing them directly. This book, instead, offers a guide to *your* gifted parenting journey. What you might experience, feel, and worry about as the parent of a gifted child. What nags at you, stumps you, and evokes your greatest concerns. What deep emotions fill you with dread and envy and regret. How to weather and even thrive despite roadblocks to your child's education, criticism based on stereotypes lobbed toward your child and toward you as a parent, and your own self-doubts. This book addresses the different challenges you likely will encounter as parent of a gifted child and recommend how to find the guidance and support you need. Tools for guiding your child based on the latest research and theory are provided. In addition, clinical examples and vignettes that highlight experiences among families of gifted children (with names and identifying information changed to protect confidentiality) are shared throughout the book.

Every parent of a gifted child has a story to tell; ask any of these parents about their fears, frustrations, and disappointments, and you will learn what they have kept hidden from view, keenly aware that most of the world at large would not understand. To learn more from *you* as parents, I recruited participants for an online survey designed to gather information about the gifted parenting experience. The survey was distributed through my professional website, my blogsite, giftedchallenges.com, various social media platforms, and some of the gifted parenting groups on those sites. Responses were obtained from 428 parents over the span of six weeks in 2022. Results are included in the Appendix section and describe the participants' family demographics, information about their child's strengths and challenges, parents' reactions and concerns related to their child's experience, and how parenting a gifted child has affected them. Responses from parents and data drawn from the survey are incorporated throughout the chapters, as well.

Keep in mind that no self-help book, no "authority figure" or "expert," and no well-meaning friend can tell you how to raise your child. Your job is to take the advice, guidance, goodwill, and information you receive along the way, decide what works, and toss aside the rest. I hope that the information and support offered throughout this book will add to that mix, but are considered within the context with what you already know about your child. To borrow a well-worn expression, *you are in the driver's seat.* However, gaining more confidence through self-awareness and support can help as you navigate this journey.

Most of all, this book will encourage and guide your own self-exploration as a parent. In the following pages, you will be asked to explore your values, assumptions, self-doubts, family of origin influences, and even some uncomfortable emotions. Of course, you might question why self-awareness is so important, especially while juggling the many daily demands of parenting. After all, you might have opened this book with the goal of better understanding your child's needs—*not* your own. Like most people, you might be hoping for some quick advice, some assured guidance, and specific tools for managing your gifted child's emotions, social struggles, or academic demands (and, yes, some of that information will be provided). *Yet, the more you understand yourself, what drives you, motivates you, and holds you back, the more you can confidently parent your gifted child.* Just as flight attendants instruct that, in case of emergency, you must place the oxygen mask on yourself before placing it on your child, you are being asked to consider your motivations, emotional reactions, and the importance of obtaining support so that you can better guide your child. You don't need a parenting emergency, though, to explore your own needs first. Understanding your thoughts, assumptions, and emotions is key to making informed decisions when faced with the everyday demands of parenting.

Chapters 1 and 2 provide an overview of giftedness, gifted education, and social and emotional challenges. Although many of you already may possess a strong knowledge base related to giftedness, the fundamentals are offered to set the stage for the remaining chapters. A solid foundation and understanding of the specific struggles parents experience when raising a gifted child should make it easier to explore, accept, and address your own personal challenges. Chapter 3 provides an overview of the process of self-exploration and Chapter 4 covers the value inherent in finding support for yourself. Chapters 5, 6, and 7 focus on specific challenges parents of the gifted face: emotions and expectations associated with pride, high expectations, envy, anxiety, regret, guilt, and disappointment. Finally, Chapter 8 addresses basic parenting skills and how these relate to raising a gifted child. While this book is not intended as a comprehensive guide to parenting, this additional parenting information should provide added support to parents already feeling stretched and challenged. Each chapter also combines clinical insights along with the latest theory and research.

Gifted children can be overwhelming, and their talents and difficulties trigger a range of emotions that are not always easy to discuss over coffee with friends. As a clinical psychologist in practice for decades, a parenting consultant, a parent of two gifted adults, and former co-chair of a gifted parent advocacy group, I have witnessed (and at times, personally experienced) the struggles, challenges, and uncertainty parents face. One thing I know to be true is that both self-awareness and support are central to making informed parenting decisions. You will find yourself approaching decisions with more sensitivity, calm, and clarity when you understand more about yourself. My hope is that any guidance and support acquired through this book will enhance your well-being and confidence along this exhilarating parenting journey.

Welcome to the exciting world of gifted parenting!

Disclaimer: Please note that written material in this book is for informational purposes only. It is not intended as clinical advice, nor a substitute for direct consultation with a psychologist, school psychologist or counselor. If you or your child would benefit from an evaluation or counseling, please seek services from a licensed mental health professional within your local community. All names and identifying information from clinical examples, vignettes, and comments derived from the Gifted Parenting Survey have been changed to preserve confidentiality.

CHAPTER ONE

What is Giftedness?

At some point, you may have suspected that your child was gifted. Perhaps they spoke before a year of age, or engaged in elaborate story-telling by age two, or were reading by age three. Maybe their Lego structures were astonishing, or they could multiply before learning to tie their shoes. You took a deep breath and wondered—*could my child be gifted?*

But then, you had your doubts. You might have questioned whether you were overreacting or getting ahead of yourself. Perhaps other children were just as capable. *Who am I to assume my child is gifted?* But you kept watch and noticed as your child continued to grasp concepts quickly, demonstrated unusually complex thinking for their age, and absorbed new information like a sponge. Still, you weren't sure. Without a clear roadmap, observations of other gifted children as a reference point, and clear guidance from experts who understand giftedness, you may have doubted your instincts.

Parents are typically quite accurate in recognizing their young child's giftedness[1]—even when they initially question their own perceptions. These observations contradict the widely held stereotype that parents frequently assume their child is gifted, and that their observations are usually wrong. Early markers of giftedness that parents notice can include heightened alertness, smiling earlier than expected, intense reactions to noise or pain, low frustration tolerance, and a decreased need for sleep[1]. Additional signs of giftedness may include intensity, a preference for novelty, high activity levels, rapid learning abilities, precocious verbal skills, and an advanced ability to form connections.

Some gifted children burst forth right out of the starting gate, displaying their precocious talents at a very young age. Others are late bloomers, or their strengths are more visual-spatial than verbal, or their passions are skewed toward only one area of interest. Parents may doubt their perceptions when developmental milestones seem to zig zag along a haphazard path. A child might be delayed with motor skills, for example, yet speak before their first birthday. Parents are most likely to question their observations when their child is neither highly verbal nor an early reader. As Silverman and Golon[1] note:

> "Children with advanced visual-spatial abilities may not be perceived as gifted by their parents or teachers unless they also demonstrate verbal precocity. When children develop speech later than their siblings, parents often worry that the children are developmentally delayed, even if they display extraordinary facility with puzzles, construction toys, creating things from odds and ends, disassembling items, and spatial memory" (p.3).

Identifying a child's gifted abilities can be clouded by a variety of developmental, learning, and social/emotional factors. Giftedness can be overlooked when a child exhibits twice exceptional (2e) conditions[2], such as when anxiety, learning disabilities, speech or motor delays, or signs of Attention Deficit/Hyperactivity Disorder (ADHD) or Autism Spectrum Disorder (ASD) coexist along with giftedness. An anxious gifted child, hesitant to speak up in class, may not be noticed. A bored gifted child who constantly chats with other students or acts out in class may receive reprimands rather than further investigation into what drives them. A gifted child with ADHD might use their intelligence to compensate for their distractibility and coast through school with average grades. As a result, their ADHD may remain hidden and untreated, and their needs as a gifted learner ignored.

Complicating the picture even further, some gifted children display social and emotional delays, where their maturity lags well behind their intellect. A five-year-old might possess the vocabulary of a teen, yet sometimes act like a toddler (often at the worst possible moments!). Asynchronous development is viewed by many as a hallmark of giftedness and is described by the National Association for Gifted Children (NAGC)[3] as a "mismatch between cognitive, emotional, and physical development of gifted individuals." These varying strengths and developmental lags confuse parents and teachers alike and confound decisions regarding school placement or options for academic acceleration.

What is giftedness?

Once you suspect that your child is highly able, gifted, or talented, you enter a shape-shifting world of definitions and terms. While all children are precious gifts to those who love them, *giftedness* is a technical term; it is a diagnostic label used to convey specific information about an individual's cognitive functioning and is used primarily in mental health and educational settings. People are different in thousands of ways; some of these differences lie in the realm of exceptional cognitive abilities. There are critics of this imperfect terminology; however, the cognitive strengths and abilities that lay the foundation for this term cannot be disputed. The definition of giftedness is separate from criteria associated with *gifted education*—a concept that varies widely, and where policies regarding how children are selected for gifted services and how those services are implemented share little consistency across school districts.

Definitions and descriptions of giftedness have taken many forms over the years. In 1916, Terman[4] defined giftedness as cognitive advancement resulting from innate abilities that were fixed over time. He expanded upon Binet and Simon's tests of "mental abilities" (initially developed to identify learning disabilities) and established use of the Stanford-Binet Intelligence Scale, a measure of cognitive abilities that could distinguish giftedness from average levels of intelligence. Most importantly, he introduced the concept of "mental age," identified through performance on the Stanford-Binet. Dividing an individual's mental age score by their chronological age, and then multiplying this number by 100, established an individual's IQ (intelligence quotient) score. Although Terman also was justifiably criticized for his racist views and the use of testing to discriminate against persons of color[5], his efforts, nonetheless, fueled an initiative to identify and understand giftedness, as well as the widespread use of the Stanford-Binet Scale—one of the most respected measures of cognitive abilities available today.

An IQ score of 130 or higher is the most commonly accepted cut-off for identifying gifted abilities. The IQ is a norms-based measure of intelligence, where an average IQ score is 100, and where most people fall within the average range of 85 to 115. A score over 130 is considered more than two standard deviations above the mean or average. This implies that less than 5% of the population possess an IQ score in the gifted range. A child's IQ score is identified through individualized cognitive or neuropsychological testing with a psychologist, neuropsychologist, or school psychologist, who are highly skilled in the use of standardized measures such as the Stanford-Binet or Wechsler Intelligence Scales. While there have been criticisms of these measures, including whether they are sensitive to cultural, ethnic, and racial differences, they are still the most widely respected tools available for evaluating cognitive functioning.

Variations in IQ scores within the gifted range of intelligence are measured by the degree of standard deviation from the mean or average. An IQ score from 130-144 is considered moderately gifted. A highly gifted score ranges from 145-159. An exceptionally gifted score ranges from 160-179, and a profoundly gifted score is 180 or above. It is not surprising that a moderately gifted child's intellectual, academic, social, and emotional needs are quite different from those of an exceptionally gifted child. A profoundly gifted child may struggle the most, as few educational settings are equipped to meet their intellectual needs.

The information derived from individualized IQ testing extends well beyond the actual IQ score, though. These tests consist of subtests that assess a variety of abilities, ranging from verbal reasoning to spatial abilities. The interplay between subtest scores—as well as the child's approach to the testing situation—provide valuable information related to strengths, weaknesses, and the presence of any learning disabilities. Contrary to popular assumptions, these individualized tests do not necessarily favor the highly verbal child, as very little writing is required; they are quite different from the paper-and-pencil achievement tests frequently administered in classroom settings. Achievement tests and other classroom-based screening measures approximate some of the information provided through formal IQ testing and can be used for prescreening large groups of students. They are useful and cost-effective tools for identifying highly able children who otherwise might have slipped through the cracks. However, these tests should be considered prescreening tools rather than definitive measures of cognitive abilities. They lack the specificity, depth, and breadth of information found in individualized cognitive testing. They also rely heavily on verbal or math skills, can overlook gifted children with strong spatial and reasoning abilities, and may be biased against English Language Learners or children raised in impoverished environments.

Controversies regarding definitions of giftedness have persisted over the years. While most would agree that a child with an IQ score of 130 or higher is gifted, there are other aspects of giftedness that these tests may overlook. Guidelines for identifying giftedness vary widely across states, counties, and school districts, and many states in the U.S.[6] lack any legal authority to require cognitive testing or to insist that gifted education is an available option in the schools. Callahan and colleagues[7] noted that: "the identification of gifted students persists as one of the most studied and controversial topics in the field. The lack of a consensus in the field on what it means to be gifted results in myriad recommendations for instruments and processes to identify gifted behaviors and students" (pp. 22-23).

Researchers and theorists have proposed criteria for gifted identification to address this controversy. Sternberg[8], for example, recommended use of the following criteria when evaluating gifted abilities:

○ "Giftedness involves more than just high IQ.

○ Giftedness has noncognitive (e.g., motivationally driven) components as well as cognitive ones.

○ Environment is crucial in terms of whether potentials for gifted performance will be realized.

○ Giftedness is not a single thing: There are multiple forms of giftedness. Hence, one-size-fits-all assessments or programs are likely to be too narrow.

○ Measures for identifying or evaluating gifted individuals need to be proposed to operationalize theories, and then they need to be evaluated rather than merely being assumed to be valid" (pp. xxiv-xxv).

Some theorists have proposed concepts that expand upon traditional views of intelligence, such as emotional intelligence[9] or the concept of multiple intelligences[10]. The role of creativity, the degree of motivation that drives expertise, and the impact of psychosocial, environmental, and emotional factors also are relevant[11-20]. Renzulli[21], for example, proposed that a definition of giftedness should encompass the following three criteria: above average intelligence, high levels of task commitment, and high levels of creativity. Creativity also was identified by many of the participants in the Gifted Parenting Survey*; 20.8% of parents indicated that their child possessed talent in art and design, and almost one-third were identified as musically talented (30.1%). Other talents also were noted, including dance, theatre, and creative writing. Many also reported that their child approached a variety of tasks with creativity: problem-solving, building, mechanical tasks, or even strategies used for debate team. Clearly, responses from this sample are consistent with other reports in the literature regarding the common thread of creativity among many gifted individuals.

The child's environment is a critical component that influences how readily their giftedness will flourish. Plomin and Stumm[22] reviewed research on the heritability of intelligence, which suggested a strong genetic component that is predictive of educational, health, and occupational outcomes. However, they also indicated that intelligence can be influenced by the environment, and that interventions in educational enrichment or dietary supplementation, for example, have an effect. Papadopolis[23], highlighted the essential interplay between gifted potential and the impact of a child's environment and summarized the following: "…the process of nurturing giftedness in children is determined by the dynamic interaction between individual strengths and a supportive environment, which can stimulate or inhibit the full use of a child's ability" (p. 305). Subotnik and colleagues[24] proposed that giftedness should be evaluated within a development context that also emphasizes the influence of the child's environment:

> "…giftedness can be viewed as developmental in that in the beginning stages, potential is the key variable; in later stages, achievement is the measure of giftedness; and in fully developed talents, eminence is the basis on which this label is granted. Psychosocial variables play an essential role in the manifestation of giftedness at every developmental stage. Both cognitive and psychosocial variables are malleable and need to be deliberately cultivated" (p. 3).

Silverman[25] has criticized theories that incorporate achievement into definitions of giftedness, as these often rely on retrospective reviews of adults who achieved success. They also overlook cultures where individual achievement is not a cultural value (e.g., where cooperation is more highly valued) and ignore the essential elements of giftedness that exist *regardless* of future accomplishments. "Recognized achievement is culturally determined; therefore, all definitions of giftedness that stem from achievement models are culturally biased" (p. 1). Silverman emphasized the importance of an education that meets a gifted child's needs, but also identified the following innate components of giftedness, each warranting recognition regardless of future achievements: an ability to readily generalize and understand abstract concepts, an inquisitive nature, advanced verbal and spatial abilities, excellent memory, a love of learning, a sophisticated sense of humor, an exceptional level of awareness and insight, passion for justice, and intensity.

In other words, if it looks like a zebra... When innate strengths are evident, *you know it when you see it.* Parents of gifted children observe these traits on a daily basis; they eventually consider the possibility of giftedness after comparisons with their child's same-age peers, or through an appreciation of normative developmental milestones. Most gifted children are not "prepped" or coached by their parents; these are kids who embrace life, learning, and creative pursuits with passion and intensity. Most parents are surprised and overwhelmed, and often are just trying to keep up with their child's latest ventures. Silverman's[25] conceptualization of giftedness reminds us that while exposure to enrichment and challenging opportunities allows these abilities to blossom, innate potential and drive are necessary components. Gifted children thrive on challenge, the spark of invention, and the joy of progressing quickly—motivating them to persist and delve deeper. This cycle of innate interest, proficiency, and further enrichment through challenging opportunities fuels growth. *But innate potential must be present.*

Many gifted children also exhibit signs of asynchronous development, where various strengths emerge at different rates and where there may be a large gap between exceptional abilities and areas of delay or weakness. This is commonly seen when there is a discrepancy between advanced academic strengths and a level of maturity far more reflective of a much younger child. Some researchers and theorists view asynchronous development as a *fundamental component of giftedness.* In fact, Silverman[25] has maintained that giftedness can be defined as "atypical development;" it is observed among young, gifted children, and its effects are stable over time. The Columbus Group's 1991 definition[26] of giftedness asserted that asynchronous development is an essential component of giftedness:

> "Giftedness is asynchronous development in which advanced cognitive abilities and heightened intensity combine to create inner experiences and awareness that are qualitatively different from the norm. This asynchrony increases with higher intellectual capacity. The uniqueness of the gifted renders them particularly vulnerable and

requires modifications in parenting, teaching, and counseling in order for them to develop optimally."

Asynchronous development can obscure a child's gifted abilities, as the
discrepancy between skills or signs of social immaturity make gifted
identification difficult. Without a clear understanding that asynchronous development is a component of giftedness, school personnel may
overlook a gifted child's strengths. Decisions related to kindergarten
start dates also may be influenced more by social maturity, especially
if grade acceleration is considered. Some parents even decide to "red
shirt" their child or delay kindergarten entry for a year to offset potential problematic social interactions. In these situations, grade or subject
acceleration can be considered at a later point. The social challenges
associated with asynchrony will be addressed further in Chapter 2.

Other definitions of giftedness have been proposed by researchers and
theorists, with a much more comprehensive discourse than is available
in this chapter[27-35]. Currently, the most widely accepted definition
of giftedness is found in the following statement from the National
Association for Gifted Children (NAGC)[32]:

> "Gifted individuals are those who demonstrate outstanding
> levels of aptitude (defined as exceptional ability to reason
> and learn) or competence (documented performance
> or achievement in top 10% or rarer) in one or more
> domains…In schools, the term gifted recognizes exception-
> ality in aptitude or achievement that requires appropriately
> differentiated services in order for the student(s) to develop
> to their potential."

The NAGC[36] also noted the critical role of environment, opportunity,
and the importance of enrichment that encourages such abilities to
flourish:

> "Students with gifts and talents perform—or have the capa-
> bility to perform—at higher levels compared to others of
> the same age, experience, and environment in one or more
> domains. They require modification(s) to their educational

experience(s) to learn and realize their potential. Students with gifts and talents:

○ Come from all racial, ethnic, and cultural populations, as well as all economic strata.

○ Require sufficient access to appropriate learning opportunities to realize their potential.

○ Can have learning and processing disorders that require specialized intervention and accommodation.

○ Need support and guidance to develop socially and emotionally as well as in their areas of talent."

What about gifted children who are not identified as gifted?

Sometimes a child's giftedness is overlooked, resulting in lost opportunities for enrichment and challenge. Just as some parents doubt their accuracy when trying to identify gifted traits, overworked teachers (or those with little training in gifted education) often fail to notice gifted children who "don't look gifted." Many gifted children do not fit stereotypes of cooperative, high achieving, and highly verbal students. Gifted children who frequently remain unidentified may be children who are quiet or shy or rambunctious, who underachieve in response to boredom, who cannot adapt to the slow, regimented pace of traditional classrooms, or whose passions are skewed toward only one area of interest. They also may be "late bloomers," whose learning trajectories seem to skyrocket from zero to sixty overnight. For example, they may show little interest in reading until they devour a chapter book of interest in one sitting. Silverman[19] claims that giftedness should be defined as atypical development; it can be observed early in life and is stable over time. In essence, what seems odd, quirky, out of sync, or downright puzzling is *quite normal* when viewed through the lens of giftedness. But many school personnel are unaware that the twisting turns of a gifted child's early development should be recognized as normative rather than viewed as a distraction or sign of disturbance that ultimately impedes gifted identification.

As noted earlier, some gifted children also possess a co-existing diagnosis, a condition often referred to as "twice exceptional,"[37] that masks their talents. Twice exceptional diagnoses may include anxiety, a learning disability, a motor-skill or sensory problem, Autism Spectrum Disorder (ASD), or Attention Deficit/Hyperactivity Disorder (ADHD). The ubiquity of these co-existing conditions has been noted in research reviews[38-40]. When any of these diagnoses are present, they may obscure identification of giftedness. Nevertheless, twice exceptional conditions are common; participants in the Gifted Parenting Survey disclosed a range of twice exceptionalities that were diagnosed by a mental health professional, physician, or specialist, such as an occupational therapist or reading specialist. In fact, 59% of participants listed one or more diagnoses related to twice exceptionality among their children, including the following: anxiety (36.9%), ADHD (25.9%), depression (15.2%), sensory processing disorder (15%), ASD (9.6%), a writing disorder, such as dysgraphia (10.3%), or a learning disability (6.8%). It should be noted that participants had the option to endorse more than one item, so some children may present with multiple conditions. In addition, when asked about their worries and concerns, parents indicated that they worry "a lot" or "always" about their child's distractibility (38.5%), organizational and time management skills (49.7%), and anxiety (52.8%). This would suggest that an even greater number of children have "sub-clinical" or undiagnosed signs of these conditions.

Gifted under-identification most commonly occurs among persons of color, children raised in impoverished environments, English Language Learners, and those who are culturally different from the school's norms[41-44]. The failure to identify giftedness in underrepresented minorities has sparked a call to action for change with how giftedness is defined and conceptualized, how gifted children are selected for enriched programming, and how gifted education is implemented[45-48]. The under-identification of gifted children within these populations has contributed to an "excellence gap"[49] where potential is neglected, enrichment is not provided, and later accomplishments never materialize. These are the children who are *most* in need of gifted services, yet rarely receive it. Peters and colleagues[48] used census-wide data to review the identification of gifted minorities and found that English Language Learners and Black, Latinx, and Native American students were disproportionately underrepresented within gifted populations. Gifted Black children often struggle with mixed messages regarding their identity and achievement, how they are perceived by others, and how to balance acceptance within their peer culture while still engaging their academic needs[49].

Some researchers have recommended using local norms to identify highly able children and expand access to gifted programming[48,52,53]. This may increase the provision of enriched services to children who may not achieve an IQ score of 130 due to the mitigating circumstances of poverty or minimal early childhood enrichment. It has been suggested that these highly able children should be recognized as capable of succeeding academically and will benefit from the challenges inherent in gifted programming. Hamilton and colleagues,[54] for example, found that school poverty predicted the percentage of gifted students identified within a school. In large school districts, those schools with the least resources had lower identification rates. "Whereas students of poverty are generally less likely to be identified for gifted services, poor students in poor schools are even less likely to be identified as gifted" (p. 6).

Children suffer when their giftedness is not acknowledged and explained to them. When schools, families, or society at large insist on denying or ignoring the concept of giftedness, children will rely on their own resources to interpret why they are so different. They might assume there is something wrong with them or feel shame about their differences. Providing a clear and thoughtful explanation merely validates what they already know to be true and places their abilities in a context they can understand. Some parents shy away from explaining giftedness to their children due to concerns that using the "gifted label" will result in an over-inflated sense of self. However, you can help your child understand their differences, appreciate that everyone has strengths and weaknesses, and recognize that giftedness does not make them "better" than anyone else[55].

Regardless of the reason for under-identification, it typically falls on you as a parent to investigate further, advocate for testing, and challenge the schools if gifted services are not provided. This role as advocate is unexpected and difficult and can evoke a range of emotions. Parenting stress associated with advocacy and finding appropriate gifted services will be addressed in later chapters throughout this book.

What is gifted education?

As noted earlier, conceptualizations of giftedness can be quite different from how gifted education is defined. Many U.S. states[6] do not require that schools offer gifted education, and even when legal mandates exist, school districts provide widely different services. Measures for identifying giftedness, criteria for entry into gifted programming, and how gifted education is defined or implemented all vary. One of the most difficult concerns parents face involves securing a challenging and meaningful education for their gifted child. Some examples of how gifted services can be provided include any of the following:

- separate classrooms for identified gifted and highly able children

- "pull-out" programs, where gifted children receive enriched instruction for one or more hours a week

- "push-in" programs, where a gifted supervisor meets with gifted children within their regular classroom or guides the classroom teacher in providing enriched instruction

- Subject or full-grade acceleration

- Online classes

- Ability grouping within the classroom, where instruction is differentiated for gifted and highly able children

- Honors or AP classes

- Dual enrollment at colleges

- Specialized schools for the gifted

○ Enriched instruction through homeschooling or homeschooling cooperatives

Gifted children experience improved self-esteem, greater engagement with learning, and improved social relationships when grouped with other gifted children. Makel and collegues[56], for example, found that even a brief, supplemental summer program with other gifted students contributed to improved academic and social self-esteem. Gifted children who are never challenged may become apathetic and start to disrespect the school's authority. Some may underachieve, drop out, and disengage completely. Others become "selective consumers"[57] who only invest their energy into those topics that interest them. Still, others coast through school with average or even above average grades, remaining well below the school's radar[58], with little motivation to challenge themselves academically. Many fail to develop essential self-regulation and executive functioning skills[59,60], such as time management, study skills, or organizational and planning skills, and are barely aware of these deficits until they eventually face challenging academic or occupational demands.

It can be argued that the well-being of gifted children is linked to their experiences at school. Ash and Huebner[61], for example, found that gifted middle school children attributed more of their "global life satisfaction" to the school climate than did children who were not identified as gifted. In other words, *school matters!* Most educators are quite aware that lack of intellectual stimulation contributes to potential academic, behavioral, and psychological problems. Yet, resistance to providing gifted services is widespread. And while caring, dedicated teachers offer many children a wonderful education, stories of disappointment still abound. Many comments from the Gifted Parenting Survey attest to these experiences. Here are a few:

> *"In 13 years of school, we only had one teacher who understood my son and tried to help. Otherwise, it was a fight the whole way."*

"I think people underestimate how much effort and time it takes to battle schools and make sure a gifted child is challenged."

"It is heartbreaking when your young child hates school so much that they become depressed."

"It took eight years to be 'heard' and have the school acknowledge my son's needs—that I wasn't pushing my son. He was racing ahead of me, and I was just trying to keep up."

"My son is twice exceptional (gifted with ASD). The public school focused on his weaknesses, but never addressed his strengths. It was incredibly frustrating that the school refused to provide advanced academic work solely on the basis of his social skills. Of course, being terribly bored in class did not help his behavior."

Schools must decide where to invest their time, energy, and financial resources. Gifted children typically comprise only a small subsection of students, and their academic needs are rarely prioritized. Parents regularly face an uphill battle when advocating within the schools, as they routinely encounter roadblocks based on financial constraints, policy considerations, and sometimes, biases and misunderstanding about the needs of gifted or highly able students. Gifted children are unfairly labeled as privileged and viewed as less deserving of academic resources than struggling or neurotypical students. Stereotypes and false assumptions are pervasive and include widespread views that gifted children "will do just fine" regardless of the educational services they receive, or that gifted education is elitist and will demoralize children who do not qualify for gifted services. In fact, almost half of participants (45.6%) in the Gifted Parenting Survey reported worrying "a lot" or "always" that adults misunderstand their child. According to Subotnik and colleagues [24]:

"The resistance is derived from the assumption that academically gifted children will be successful no matter what educational environment they are placed in, and because their families are believed to be more highly educated and hold above-average access to human capital wealth. These arguments run counter to psychological science indicating the need for all students to be challenged in their schoolwork and that effort and appropriate educational programming, training and support are required to develop a student's talents and abilities" (p. 3).

Recent trends that seek to eliminate "tracking" in schools (where children are placed in an academic level and are unable to move vertically to different levels) have attempted to address minority bias and discrimination. Sweeping changes to eliminate tracking in many schools have been initiated; however, these efforts also eliminate enrichment opportunities for gifted minority children or those from impoverished backgrounds. Regardless of intentions, purposely holding back gifted and highly able children from a meaningful education punishes these children, especially since their families may lack the financial resources to provide supplementary enrichment opportunities. As Silverman[25] has stated: "You can't sweep away developmental differences with political ideologies...these differences need to be recognized, evaluated, understood, and accommodated through differentiated services and programs" (p. 1).

Participants in the Gifted Parenting Survey expressed strong concerns regarding their child's academic experiences. When asked what they worry about as parents, 60.2% of parents indicated that they worry "a lot" or "always" about whether their child is receiving a challenging education. Only 5.6% of this sample claimed that they never worry about this. Furthermore, parents indicated that they worry "a lot" or "always" about their child's boredom or disengagement from school (59.1%), underachievement (34.3%), and limited opportunities to challenge themselves (41.1%). They also reported worrying "a lot" or "always" about whether their child would reach their potential (53.5%) or find a meaningful career (38.3%). As one parent commented:

> *"Exceptionally few resources are allocated for gifted children, and this seems like backwards thinking. The return on*

investment in these children is incalculable. What these kids can offer society as adults is worth every penny of investment in childhood…It is incredibly frustrating to navigate school systems that are not only disinterested in identifying and fostering growth in these kids, but which often find these kids' needs to be a nuisance."

Ideally, schools can support children who possess a wide range of abilities. *All* children deserve a challenging education that meets their academic, developmental, and social/emotional needs. Gifted children deserve the same consideration as their neurotypical peers. Unfortunately, the burden of advocacy often falls on parents. Your willingness to challenge the system and to advocate for your child's needs is essential. Much work is needed going forward so that these complex and difficult issues are addressed—but you are equipped to tackle the challenge!

What's next?

Understanding what makes your gifted child tick involves more than acquiring knowledge about intellectual giftedness and the role of gifted education. Parents also must consider the social and emotional challenges commonly seen among the gifted. The following chapter addresses these concerns, through an overview of social and emotional characteristics that is supported by research and theory. An awareness of these factors sets a framework for delving into *your* self-awareness, which is covered in the remaining chapters.

*The Gifted Parenting Survey was initiated online with the intention of gathering more information about the parents' experience. Data and quotes are drawn from the 428 parents who responded to the survey. Information related to their child's giftedness also is included. To ensure confidentiality, quotes taken from the survey do not include any personal or identifying information. Please see the Appendix for a full summary of the survey.

CHAPTER TWO

The Social and Emotional Aspects of Giftedness

Many families quickly learn that giftedness must be considered through the lens of social and emotional functioning. Exceptional intellectual strengths often infuse a level of intensity, empathy, and sensitivity that affects thoughts, emotions, and interactions with others. Passion and focus are hallmark characteristics of a gifted child immersed in what is most meaningful to them. Intensity can light a spark of joy when delving into a new project or evoke compassion for those less fortunate. Sometimes, though, intensity can spiral into negative thoughts and moods. Children with highly active minds can fixate on worries and fears; sensitivity can evolve into existential angst or despair. McDowell[1] has pointed out that approaches to understanding giftedness that focus solely on intellectual abilities or academic achievement ignore the traits most parents of gifted children readily describe, such as heightened sensitivity and emotional reactivity (often categorized as overexcitabilities). Roeper[2] has commented that gifted people possess "a greater awareness, a greater sensitivity, and a greater ability to understand and transform perceptions into intellectual and emotional experiences" (p. 21). Clearly, the social and emotional aspects of giftedness must be considered when evaluating, teaching, and parenting gifted children.

Living with Intensity

Research, theory, and clinical observations have identified a range of personality and psychological traits that coexist with gifted intellectual strengths, and highlight the prevalence of sensitivity, emotional reactivity, and intensity[2-6]. While intensity can be challenging and exhausting, it also infuses family interactions with energy and exuberance. Participants in the Gifted Parenting Survey corroborated these findings, as a large proportion of parents indicated that their children exhibited emotional intensity (80.8%) and heightened sensitivity (72.7%). They also highlighted both the joys and challenges associated with heightened intensities:

> *"I often wonder what dinnertime conversations are like in other households. In ours, they can bounce from some new science theory someone read about to reminding our teenagers to use silverware (still!) to etymology to glares from one kid because their sibling is chewing noisily to discussions on which religion is best to one kid teaching the other how to swear in Latin. It's exhilarating but exhausting!"*

> *"Living with the intensity is for me the hardest part to balance. It feels like from the moment they wake up until the moment they go to sleep, we join them on a roller coaster that keeps going. No stops. However, there is also so much joy in seeing all the creative ways they try to problem-solve. It is an exhausting, yet very joyful journey at the same time."*

> *"Such immense joy and heartbreak: enthusiasm and exhaustion. The words 'insatiable' and 'constant energy' often come to mind when I describe what it can be like."*

The concept of "overexcitabilities" has become an umbrella term used to describe gifted children's intensities. Dabrowski proposed the term (within the context of his theory of positive disintegration) and identified five forms of overexcitabilities: psychomotor, sensual, intellectual, imaginational, and emotional[7-11]. Most parents of gifted children can attest to their child's intensity in at least in one of these five areas. As one participant in the Gifted Parenting Survey noted:

> *"It's similar to parenting typical kids, but with that added 'extra' to everything. So, think about all the aspects of a*

person—the physical, spiritual, emotional psychological—and then amplify the intensity of those, and you get the gifted child. I suppose it's those 'overexcitabilities' that Dabrowski spoke of in his theory. For a parent, it's exhausting. I think that gifted kids are very much special needs kids, in that they should be able to receive services to meet their needs, just the same as children who receive IEP's [individualized education plans] for their special needs."

Nevertheless, the concept of overexcitabilities is not a diagnostic or mental health term, and its relevance has been questioned due to inconsistent research findings[12-13]. Overexcitabilities have been shown to overlap with ADHD[14] and they correspond with greater Openness to Experience[15,16], one of the personality factors identified in the highly researched Five Factor Model of Personality[17]. Like many other personality measures that characterize immutable traits, the concept of overexcitabilities may be helpful for highlighting the general level of emotional intensity among gifted people, but it lacks specificity and risks pigeonholing emotions and behaviors into rigid and stable traits. At best, the concept affirms the importance of recognizing emotional intensity as a central component of giftedness and can be a springboard for further research.

Asynchronous Development

As noted in Chapter 1, gifted children commonly exhibit signs of asynchronous development. While it can manifest as a large gap between strengths and areas of weakness, it is most problematic when the child's maturity is more reflective of what is usually observed in a much younger child. Difficulties with social relationships and behavioral immaturity can result in social rejection from peers as well as disapproval from adults. And sensitive gifted children are especially likely to struggle emotionally when they feel rejected and misunderstood.

The parenting challenges inherent in raising an asynchronous gifted child cannot be overstated. Parents are frequently astonished as they watch their child career from precocious to regressive behavior within seconds. Both Alsop[20] and Silverman[21] have noted that asynchronous development is one of the greatest challenges parents face. The uncertainty associated with wondering "which child will show up today—and what age will they be" keeps families on alert and adds to their stress. Tolan[22] claimed that "gifted children are on a developmental trajectory that is outside of norms from infancy onward. They reach recognized milestones of development on a schedule that is unique to them, putting them out of sync with society's expectations. In addition, they may be out of sync internally, with cognitive, social, and emotional development on separate and sometimes quite different timetables." (p. 2). She further commented that:

> "The young gifted child may appear to be many ages at once. He may be eight (his chronological age) when riding a bicycle, twelve when playing chess, fifteen when studying algebra, ten when collecting fossils, and two when asked to share his chocolate chip cookie with his sister. This variability in behavior and perception is difficult for parents and schools to handle and difficult for the child as well" (p. 2).

It is not surprising then that two-thirds of parents in the Gifted Parenting Survey (65.9%) claimed that their child exhibited signs of asynchronous development. They also reported struggles with social immaturity (45.3%) and executive functioning skills (58.4%) — challenges often seen among asynchronous gifted children. Some parents shared the following anecdotes:

> "By second grade, my son was identified as gifted, but the struggles with relating to peers, lack of strong friendships and being behind his peers in emotional and social maturity became evident. He struggled in unstructured environments such as the playground, even though he is exceptionally athletic, but it was the social aspect that challenged him. Then he began getting bullied at school. It was heartbreaking to watch my son go through this."

> "I have found that the asynchronous development has continued. My daughter is 18. She is highly skilled at creative

*writing and English Literature, but is still extremely attached
to a favorite soft toy, using it to help with her anxiety."*

Silverman[3] provided an apt description of what many parents observe
with their asynchronous gifted child:

> "Asynchrony is composed of advanced cognition, inten-
> sity, uneven development, feeling out-of-sync with peers,
> unusual awareness, complexity, and vulnerability. Uneven
> development is a universal characteristic of giftedness. The
> child develops mentally at a much faster rate than physi-
> cally. She contemplates the meaning of life, but she can't
> tie her shoes. He can discuss black holes with ease, but he
> hasn't figured out how to hold his pencil" (p. 2).

Silverman further asserted that asynchrony is an even greater challenge
for parents of highly gifted children:

> The higher the child's IQ, the greater the asynchrony.
> Greater asynchrony means greater vulnerability. The more
> the child differs from the norm in either direction, the
> more difficult it will be to fit in, to belong, to get one's
> needs met in a regular public school classroom. Children
> four standard deviations below the norm are not in regular
> classrooms. It is questionable if the regular classroom can
> meet the needs of children four standard deviations above
> the norm. (p. 3).

How intensity and emotional reactivity affect psychological well-being

Questions have been raised regarding whether gifted children are more
prone to psychological problems than their neurotypical peers. Some
of you may have socially mature, well-adjusted, and easy-going gifted
children, who exhibit no signs of distress. They have adapted well to
the resources and limitations within their schools, show leadership
qualities, and make friends easily. However, others reading this may
be navigating mental health crises with their children, or at least must
manage the tumultuous impact of their intensities. Some researchers

and theorists view gifted intellectual strengths as a buffering mechanism that protects them from distress. Others propose that their heightened emotional reactivity leaves them vulnerable. Neihart and Yeo[18] summarized this debate by noting that research supports both perspectives:

> Generally, two views have prevailed. The first view proposes that gifted children as a group are better adjusted than their typically developing peers because they are capable of greater understanding of self and others. Therefore, they cope better with stress and conflicts…The second view suggests that gifted children are more at-risk for psychological problems, particularly during adolescence and adulthood, because they are more sensitive to interpersonal conflicts and experience greater degrees of alienation and stress. (p. 497).

The powerful emotions many gifted children and adults feel can enhance their lives, as they passionately immerse themselves in compelling interests and engage in creative expression. Witnessing our child's growth and development can be a joy. As one parent in the Gifted Parenting Survey expressed: *"While I worry a lot about the day-to-day—watching my child's brain engage and soar fills me with wonder and hope."* On the other hand, too much intensity or emotional reactivity can contribute to distressing symptoms or behaviors. Parents of gifted children frequently bemoan their child's exhausting level of energy, anxiety, perfectionism, paralyzing self-doubt, overthinking, social anxiety, meltdowns over seemingly routine situations, or distress over social justice or existential issues. Participants in the Gifted Parenting Survey claimed that their child exhibited the following examples of intensity: perfectionism (67.8%), existential concerns (46.5%), and empathy (50%). They also indicated that their children experienced levels of anxiety (36.9%) and depression (15.2%) that have been diagnosed by mental health professionals.

Silverman[3] has suggested that gifted teens and adults are more susceptible to developing psychological problems due to their sensitivity to interpersonal conflict and the likelihood that they experience greater levels of stress and alienation from others. Many gifted children learn to hide their giftedness, tone down their intensity, and suppress their sense of self to fit in with peers. Silverman noted that: "they are the only exceptionality that can pretend to be like everyone else" (p. 6). Although seemingly adaptive, the drive to fit in takes its toll, as gifted children and teens may feel like impostors, further increasing their disengagement from others. Psychological distress may result from the cumulative impact of disengagement, alienation, and mistreatment from peers—rather than from internal or biologically mediated psychological problems. Participants in the Gifted Parenting Survey voiced concerns about their child's social experiences and indicated that they worry "a lot" or "always" about their social immaturity (34.8%), their experience of rejection or bullying (29.9%), and their ability to fit in with peers (53.3%).

> *"It is isolating having a gifted child who has a hard time finding people who have strong interests at such a young age. My son constantly asks, 'Mom are there any other kids out there who like science as much as I do? I ask kids what they are interested in and they say I don't know yet.'"*

> *"I worry about him 'fitting in' with other kids his age He is so impulsive that he often dominates conversations without realizing it and can have emotional outbursts that confound other adults and kids. They don't understand how someone so bright and articulate could have immature outbursts."*

> *"My child has an extremely high IQ but is extraordinarily behind socially and emotionally. Diagnosed with ADHD, ASD and Anxiety Disorder, my son is constantly struggling in a world that was not set up for him...I can imagine the frustration he must feel when he is thinking about the world around him on such a higher level than his peers and even most adults."*

Interestingly, although participants in the survey expressed concerns (noted in Chapter 1) about the school's limitations and how other adults react to their child, relatively few parents reported worrying "a lot" or "always" about whether their child would disrespect authority (19.1%). Despite their child's experience in a world where many adults do not understand them, most of the children in this sample continue to behave respectfully toward authority figures.

Parents of gifted children are often troubled when they witness so much emotional intensity and upheaval. Many feel worried and heartbroken that their child is burdened by these intense emotions. Parents in the Gifted Parenting Survey indicated that they worry "a lot" or "always" about their child's intensity (51.2%), sensitivity (41.3%), anxiety (52.8%), perfectionism (46.5%), depression (25%), overthinking (49.8%), and whether they will find happiness in the future (49.5%). It should be noted that more parents expressed concerns about their child's level of depression or anxiety than when asked if these conditions were diagnosed by a licensed mental health professional. It is possible that some gifted children experience a subclinical degree of distress that does not meet criteria for a diagnosable disorder. Nevertheless, the child still is enduring enough distress that their parents are worried about them. Many of the parents also attributed their child's emotional struggles to their negative experiences at school or their approach to academic expectations. The following are examples from the survey:

> *"Sending him to school is traumatizing to him but I'm left with little options for a 2e child. School doesn't get it. He feels discouraged and depressed for every week that he goes to school. Hates learning at school, while knowledge and curiosity dominate his life at home. Others feel confused and question his giftedness because of his emotional challenges."*

> *"My child was one of the highest achievers in her gifted elementary school. I spent so much time trying to teach her that she doesn't have to do her best work on every assignment. Perfectionism stressed her out and took so much time. I felt like I was possibly the only parent who had to teach their child to do quick, sloppy work (and still get a perfect grade from the teacher!)."*

Developing a sense of self—in a world not geared toward the gifted

The young, gifted child's precocious questions and curiosity continue throughout childhood and are amplified as they approach adolescence. Many question their religious and family values, rage against injustice, and refuse to conform if certain rules seem pointless. Szymanski[19] has pointed out that gifted teens question their values and their sense of self as they attempt to form an identity separate from their role within the family. Webb[24] also noted the prevalence of distress as gifted teens struggle with existential issues. They ponder the meaning of life and examine their family's values, and may feel disenfranchised and despairing as they question beliefs that they previously thought were true. These hurdles are so common among gifted teens that they could be considered a normal part of their developmental trajectory; although distressing, grappling with personal identity and existential issues eventually may foster greater clarity related to their sense of self.

Szymanski[19] summarized research on emotional concerns among gifted children and adolescents, including their emerging sense of identity. She reported findings that gifted students frequently possess a higher academic self-concept, but lower social, physical, and athletic self-concepts when compared with non-gifted peers. She highlighted the social and emotional concerns common among gifted children and emphasized that supporting the "whole child" — including their emotional needs — is critical to nurturing a gifted child. She proposed a harmony/disharmony hypothesis to describe how giftedness affects all aspects of a child's life:

> "The harmony hypothesis supposes that high IQ allows individuals access to better problem-solving abilities, greater frequency of ideas, and abstract thinking, which serve as buffers to reduce some negative social and emotional issues faced in development. Conversely, the disharmony hypothesis posits that feelings of being different, increased awareness, and pressure to perform may contribute to a more negative developmental experience for gifted children than for nongifted" (p. 417).

Even those gifted children who are not emotionally distressed or warrant a mental health diagnosis often struggle to fit into a world not necessarily built for them. Their heightened sensitivity, concerns about injustice, and outside-the-box thinking sometimes makes them ill-suited for traditional roles. Just as many gifted children struggle to fit into traditional classrooms or peer social gatherings, gifted adults also may question their decisions, struggle to conform, have difficulty finding like-minded peers, and do not pursue traditional career paths. Many have multiple talents, a disposition often referred to as multipotentiality, and must choose a career path that may leave other talents behind. These differences make life more challenging. Silverman[3] poignantly described the dilemmas gifted adults face when searching to find a place where they fit:

> "Many gifted individuals do not fit well into society. They cannot "play the game" and pretend to be something they're not. Sensitive to injustice, they cannot ignore the power plays and moral infractions. Many gifted adults leave corporate America to set up their own businesses — not to make more money, but because they would have had to sacrifice their moral integrity if they stayed…The intensity, perfectionism, complexity, and sensitivity of this population are actually disadvantages in societies where these traits are not valued (pp. 6-7).

Are the gifted *predisposed* to emotional difficulties?

Highly gifted individuals also may be predisposed to the development of psychological and even physical problems that could arise under certain (as yet undetermined) conditions. Recently, Karpinski and colleagues[25] summarized the literature on heightened sensitivity and cognitive, emotional, and physiological reactivity, and conducted research to study this topic further. They surveyed highly gifted individuals and compared their self-reported claims of psychological and physical symptoms with national norms. Study participants reported a greater number of symptoms associated with anxiety and mood disorders, ADHD, ASD, and physiological diagnoses, such as asthma, allergies, and autoimmune disease, which was consistent with other findings in the literature. The researchers summarized their results as suggestive of a "hyper brain/hyper body" model that reflects the impact of giftedness on various levels of functioning. They concluded that high IQ is "a potential risk factor for affective disorders [mood disorders such as depression], ADHD, ASD, and for increased incidence of disease related to immune dysregulation" (p. 8). The association between high levels of giftedness and immune responsivity is striking, as it implicates an underlying nervous system reactivity that affects gifted individuals on a cognitive, emotional, *and* physiological level. Drawing from the field of psychoneuro-immunology, the researchers highlighted the impact of heightened physiological reactivity:

> "For highly intelligent individuals with overexcitabilities, even normal stimuli such as a clothing tag or a common but unnatural sound can become physically painful. Continuous seemingly minor insults such as these may mimic a low level, chronic stress which can eventually launch an inappropriate immune response. As with other environmental threats, like an infection or toxin, the body believes it is in danger. When the sympathetic nervous system becomes chronically activated, it finds itself in a continuous fight, flight, or freeze state, which triggers a series of changes in the brain and the body that can dysregulate immune function" (p. 9).

Although the association between giftedness and psychological/physiological reactivity may be evident for many gifted individuals, caution is needed with respect to determining how symptoms and behaviors are assessed, and when a diagnosis is warranted. Unfortunately, when some educators or health care providers are faced with a gifted child's behavioral problems or emotional distress, they may reflexively propose a label or psychiatric diagnosis that does not consider how giftedness influences the behavior. Gifted children may receive a misdiagnosis of ADHD, ASD, OCD (obsessive-compulsive disorder), or an anxiety disorder, when in fact, their symptoms are more consistent with the emotional intensity, sensitivity, heightened energy, rigidity, asynchronous development, or overthinking so prevalent among gifted children and adolescents[26]. What also can be overlooked is how a child's distress may be influenced by peer rejection, apathy associated with boredom at school, or internal pressure to succeed, rather than internal or biologically mediated psychological problems (such as a chemical imbalance). At worst, some diagnostic terms are used in a dismissive or pejorative manner. And sometimes, professionals who are not qualified to make a diagnosis still suggest a diagnostic label, which may trigger unnecessary anxiety among parents. *"You might want to get your child checked out for ADHD." "Your child has such difficulty with the other kids. Have you considered whether he might be autistic?"* Even when diagnoses are provided with the best of intentions, generalizations, and stereotypes about the gifted can influence what observers actually "see" when formulating an understanding of their behavior. The following examples from the Gifted Parenting Survey highlight what can occur when giftedness and co-existing mental health or learning conditions are not fully understood:

> *"My child was suspected to be autistic in pre-K. After the evaluation, he was identified as profoundly gifted with no signs of autism. He was just shutting himself out in class."*

> *"My child disengaged from school... We discovered through further independent evaluation that a non-verbal learning disability (NVLD) is part of the equation. [There were] six years of schooling from when my youngest was identified GT [gifted and talented] to when NVLD was diagnosed, and no related supports/accommodations or services were present because the GT piece masked the neurodiversity."*

Clearly, gifted children, teens, and adults deserve a comprehensive evaluation when psychological symptoms are present—one that respects their felt experience and is considered within the context of asynchrony, sensitivities, and external societal pressures associated with "life as gifted." It is likely that gifted individuals experience the same psychological conditions as their neurotypical peers; however, giftedness infuses an added layer of awareness, introspection, and sensitivity that may trigger or intensify their reactions. An active mind can wander off in a variety of directions. Moods can be amplified by an abundance of sensitivity and empathy. Sensitive children can feel especially wounded by social rejection or teachers who chastise them when they voice their ideas. However, emotional distress should never be dismissed as "just due to giftedness" and then ignored. Regardless of whether a child receives a psychiatric diagnosis, a misdiagnosis, or if their symptoms result from gifted over-reactivity, *their distress is real* and should be acknowledged and addressed. Your child's pediatrician, school counselor, or school psychologist are excellent resources for finding referrals to local mental health professionals or other specialists, such as speech or occupational therapists. Intensity, overthinking, an active mind, and powerful emotions can be overwhelming; it can be tough to turn down the intensity volume on that radio dial! Expert professionals with clarity about the impact and overlay of giftedness on psychological functioning are best positioned to clarify diagnostic issues and provide guidance.

The information in this chapter that suggests greater emotional reactivity and a possible predisposition to psychological difficulties is not meant to alarm you. Gifted people do not hold any exclusive rights to distress! Anyone can struggle with mental health concerns or any of the intense emotions listed above. And many gifted children breeze through childhood, harness the power of their intense and active minds toward what interests them, and can brush off slights and disappointments with a shrug. Nevertheless, even seemingly well-adjusted gifted kids still observe and process unfairness in the world around them, experience personal disappointments, and are aware of their differences. The propensity toward greater emotional reactivity among *some* gifted children, though, suggests that as parents, we must step up our game to provide as much support, calming reassurance, and encouragement as possible. This includes providing a safe, loving environment, necessary limits, and an expectation that they will be resilient and capable of weathering tough challenges. We cannot prevent some of the disappointments, misery, or even trauma they may encounter in life; however, we can help them develop the coping strategies and a grounded sense of self to endure and even thrive under difficult conditions. More about parenting strategies will be addressed in Chapter 8.

Recognizing and understanding your child's intensities and emotional struggles is essential to your own self-discovery. Your reactions to your child's emotions may spark a personal recognition of your own struggles from childhood, as many parents of gifted children are gifted as well. You may feel sadness and empathy as you watch your child struggle, and acknowledge that you, too, endured the same travails when you were young. You also might struggle with these intensities well into the present. The compassionate recognition that your child's emotional intensity is both heartrending and yet quite familiar, offering you greater insight and perspective into their experience. You may know what it was like to feel different from others, or endure rejection from peers, or languish, bored in classrooms never designed for what you needed. Gaining greater understanding of your reactions to your child's struggles is essential, and will be discussed in the remaining chapters.

What's next?

The overviews in Chapters 1 and 2 cover some of the basic concepts and issues associated with giftedness. Keep in mind, though, that *each* child, *each* adult, and *each* family are different. Take what you have read here, along with the research and theoretical views referenced, and consider how it relates to your situation. Some aspects of giftedness will fit for you or your child; others will not. As you explore your parenting journey, you may experience a range of feelings, reactions, worries, and joys, yet find that there are few opportunities to share and explore your emotions. The following chapters will address topics related to understanding and working with your personal reactions, how to access support from others who understand your concerns, and how to use self-awareness and a deeper appreciation of your parenting role along this journey.

CHAPTER THREE

The Essential Importance
of Self-Awareness

Given the daily responsibilities parents face, achieving greater self-awareness may seem like an afterthought—another task at the bottom of a long to-do list. Why take the time to focus on yourself when there is so much to do? You might feel a little guilty about even acknowledging your emotions, and perhaps, feel undeserving of time spent focusing on you. *Who am I to complain? My child is gifted—that's a wonderful thing...right?* With so many parents clamoring to place their child into a gifted program, it might seem odd that assuming *the role of parent of a gifted child* would be difficult. After all, why would anyone resist or resent or even feel downright panic over this new role? Yet, like many other parents of gifted children, you might feel overwhelmed, confused, ambivalent, or resentful about the added responsibilities that accompany these challenges.

Understanding your reactions and feelings—and why this is so important

Every parent experiences a depth of emotions toward their children that is hard to quantify. The stunning, tearful embrace when you greet your newborn for the first time. The desperate end-of-your-rope frustration at 3:00 AM with a colicky baby. The blissful, ethereal calm with your snuggling toddler. The rage that catches in your throat after your 3-year-old says "no" for the 20th time. Parents of young children are awash in emotions and often respond instinctively to momentary events. This automatic reactivity can work well in a crisis or when

juggling three tasks at a time. But an absence of self-reflection sometimes leads to habitual behavior patterns. All of us are influenced by
underlying wishes, fears, and dreams. Long-held attitudes and assumptions about children, social norms, and parenting philosophies shape
our behaviors, and family of origin experiences can either overtly or
unconsciously influence decisions. When behaviors and responses are
initiated without much consideration and thoughtfulness, though,
you may not achieve the outcome you want. Parenting based solely
upon instinct and knee-jerk reactions, minus clarity about your values
and guiding principles, is like driving without a roadmap.

Parents of gifted children are just as susceptible to underlying emotions
and family of origin influences as any other parent. They can easily
succumb to social pressure and guidelines from books, media, and
reports about the latest parenting trends. Since parents of gifted
children often have few available resources to help them place their
emotions in context, they may feel guilty or ashamed of their feelings,
and struggle in isolation. As a result, their actions may lack a clear
path that is consistent with their values.

> *Mara struggled with her highly active, twice exceptional gifted*
> *child who was diagnosed with ADHD. She felt overwhelmed,*
> *and at one point, reached down to slap him. She stopped*
> *herself when she saw the terror in his eyes. Mommy was out*
> *of control, and this upset him almost as much as the threat*
> *of being hit. When she regrouped and the storm had passed,*
> *she recalled some childhood memories. She remembered how*
> *readily her parents would spank her, how frightening it was at*
> *first, but then, how she steeled herself in the face of impending*
> *punishment. Mara adapted by no longer sharing feelings with*
> *her parents and did whatever she could to hide anything that*
> *might cause conflict. Despite how distressing these childhood*
> *experiences were, she had lapsed into an automatic repetition of*
> *her parents' behaviors. She did not want to repeat this pattern*
> *with her son and vowed to stay on top of her anger and learn*
> *other disciplinary techniques that would not push him away.* *

Self-awareness is key. When we respond unconsciously to powerful emotions, we rarely parent at our best. Just as flight attendants instruct us to put the oxygen mask on first before assisting a young child, we need to fortify ourselves with the confidence and strength to best support our children. It is human nature to avoid what is uncomfortable. It is hard to face our insecurity, worries and regrets. It is equally painful to review what we learned from our family of origin and realize that some of our parents' decisions were flawed. Self-awareness is neither a luxury nor an indulgence—understanding our emotions and values takes hard work. However, when we recognize, understand, compassionately accept, and then learn from our reactions and underlying emotions, we are better equipped to make sound decisions.

The challenges inherent in raising a gifted child differ from what might be experienced within families of neurotypical children, and can contribute to a somewhat different family environment. Silverman and Golon[1], for example, described a variety of characteristics commonly found among families of the gifted. These include increased sensitivity, intensity, argumentativeness (likened to "mental sparring"), humor, perfectionism, conscientiousness, complex emotions, the ability to view problems from multiple perspectives, cohesiveness, a lack of conventionality, a desire to be understood, and a strong drive for meaning. Webb[2] also observed that families of the gifted often possess an appreciation of existential concerns and curiosity about the meaning of life. These commonalities create a different interpersonal dynamic than what exists among many other families.

While some parents readily acknowledge anxiety about their gifted child's academic progress or worries about peer relationships, many are reluctant to admit to the more complicated and distressing emotions that may lurk inside: those dark, unspoken, nagging wishes and fears that lie just beneath the surface. Frequently ignored and sometimes unconscious, those underlying emotions and behaviors can impede parenting efforts. Envy, shame, bitterness, regret, and guilt are no stranger to most parents of gifted children. Competitive strivings, overinvolvement, projection of hopes and dreams, and ambivalence also may come into play. This additional aspect of the gifted parenting journey—the sobering jolt of reality when these hidden emotions surface—may take you completely by surprise.

How do these emotions affect you?

The underlying attitudes and emotions noted above may influence decisions without your full consent. In essence, you may be functioning on autopilot and responding instinctively to your child's behaviors. It is commonplace, though, to avoid self-reflection, especially when you risk discovering unpleasant memories or negative feelings. We may not like what we uncover and cringe when recalling past behavior we regret. We might become furious toward those we felt were unjust or uncaring. We might even worry that traumatic childhood experiences or conflicts with our parents will affect our current parenting capabilities. Yet, taking stock of past influences, understanding how these might affect us, and working to act differently with our own children *is within our control.* By digging deeper and truly understanding your feelings and motivations, you gain perspective and will likely avoid taking actions that might negatively affect you or your child. Once self-awareness increases, whether through self-reflection, self-education, or conversations with trusted peers, you can gain control over how these emotions affect you. Parenting authors Siegel and Hartzell[3] stress the importance of achieving self-awareness:

> "Understanding our lives can free us from the otherwise almost predictable situation in which we recreate the damage to our children that was done to us in our own childhoods. Research has clearly demonstrated that our children's attachment to us will be influenced by what happened to us when we were young if we do not come to process and understand those experiences" (p. 19).

As mentioned above, parenting without self-awareness is like driving without a roadmap. We fall back on sometimes ineffective or harmful family of origin practices, respond in a flash to momentary stressors, and ultimately feel even more overwhelmed. Parents of gifted children often experience unique parenting challenges that intensify the demands of their job. Recognizing what reactions and emotions arise is the first step. Reaching out for support from those you trust is another essential step toward self-awareness and confidence in your parenting decisions and cushions the blow from any troubling self-discovery. The following sections of this chapter highlight some of the common challenges parents of gifted children face.

The daunting responsibility of raising a gifted child

Although you may be overjoyed to find that your child is gifted, a nagging sense of anxiety may arise. The burden of raising a gifted child—with their boundless energy, sensitivity, curiosity, and quirks—can feel overwhelming. *Am I handling all of this correctly? How do I know if I am doing the right thing?* This daunting sense of responsibility can evoke fear that every decision is precarious and fraught with significance, and that any misstep has the potential to derail your child's development. And while most parents eventually settle in and realize that their best efforts are good enough and that perfection is never required, doubts may remain. As noted in Chapter 2, gifted children present an array of challenges that take their toll. Heightened sensitivities, asynchronous development, intense emotions, anxiety, high energy, and perfectionism are common. In her dissertation research on parents of gifted children, Rimlinger[4] found that when gifted children exhibited problematic behaviors such as oppositionality (e.g., frequent, defiant behavior), parents experienced greater levels of anxiety and stress. Of course, oppositional behaviors are likely problematic for any family. But when coupled with the challenges and demands associated with giftedness and limited support from schools, parents can feel overwhelmed.

Do some of the following questions sound familiar?

- ○ What does it take to nurture my gifted child?

- ○ What if I make a mistake—and either push too hard or not enough?

- ○ Am I solely responsible for ensuring that my child's potential is achieved?

○ How do I ensure that my child has a "normal" childhood and is not hurt along the way?

○ Am I up to the task?

○ How will my life change with these added responsibilities?

It is not surprising that parents can feel overwhelmed with this new role. They often feel uncertain and isolated as they raise their sometimes emotionally intense or highly sensitive child with few clear guidelines available. Parenting is a complicated journey for any family: joyous, yet full of unexpected challenges. Giftedness infuses parenting with even more complex questions and choices. Addressing these situations might seem full of potential pitfalls and may challenge your sense of competence as a parent. Nevertheless, basic parenting principles are the best guidelines to follow when faced with these unique challenges. These include loving support for your child's emotional and intellectual needs, providing a safe and trusting family environment, setting appropriate limits, and tailoring interactions to your child's developmental level. (More about parenting practices can be found in Chapter 8.) Jolly and Matthews[5], in their review of available research on parents of gifted children, summarized the following reassuring conclusions:

> "Effective parents of children of all ages encourage their children to ask questions and use their imaginations through play; they react to their child in a developmentally appropriate manner, and they allow their young high-ability children to make decisions commensurate with their age. At younger ages, in their capacity as their child's first teacher, these parents gauge their child's ability level and motivation and are highly engaged with their children in family activities. These parents report engaging their children in intellectual activities more often than parents of average ability children do, and they also report supporting independence, encouraging the development of a sense of responsibility, and providing unconditional love and support for their child" (pp. 272-273).

Advocacy wherever you go

An unexpected demand on your time involves advocacy, along with adjustment to your newfound role as an advocate. You never asked for this responsibility. Yet, you find yourself in the role of *ambassador for giftedness* wherever you go—explaining, clarifying, and sometimes apologizing for your gifted child's behavior. This can happen anywhere: at the soccer field, the check-out line, Thanksgiving dinner with relatives, *and* at parent-teacher conferences. It falls on you to explain your child's sometimes unusual behaviors, and how giftedness or twice exceptional issues are displayed. Many of the adults in your child's life may have little understanding of giftedness. Your child's classroom teacher, pediatrician, coach, music teacher, camp counselor, religious activities leader, and just about anyone else you encounter often require an education in the fundamentals of giftedness. Providing that crucial information might sound something like this:

> *Yes, he is bright, and sounds like a 10-year-old. But he has something called "asynchronous development" which means that his emotions are way behind his intellect. So, I know it seems like he should be more mature, but sometimes he has meltdowns and acts like a four-year-old. Trust me, it's just part of his development and we're working on it.*

In addition, you are responsible for ensuring that your child receives a fair and appropriate education. Not the school…*you*. Yes, of course, the school district is obligated to educate your child. But the academic needs of gifted children are deemed a low priority. Since gifted education is not legally mandated in some states in the U.S.[6], parents possess little authority when requesting additional services. As noted in Chapter 1, the crisis in how gifted education is implemented and the dearth of gifted services are pervasive problems, regardless of whether this stems from limited professional training, outright refusal to provide services, lack of clarity regarding the equitable identification and implementation of gifted services, or philosophical debates that ignore the benefits of ability grouping or academic acceleration[7-13]. Resistance is common and requests are considered at the whim of the school's leadership. While many teachers are sympathetic to this dilemma and would like to provide enriched instruction, even the most well-meaning teachers must juggle the competing demands of a roomful of students with diverse academic abilities. You will need to find in-roads, pick your battles, and determine when to compromise… and when to throw in the towel and consider different educational options, if financially feasible.

> *Linda felt devastated. She had spoken with her daughter's teacher, who claimed there was no time during the day when individualized instruction could be provided. She went to the principal, and eventually to the school board, and nothing could be done. She eventually decided to work part-time and homeschool her daughter, even though this created a financial hardship for her family.*

Ironically, some parents of twice exceptional gifted children find that the school receives them with open arms. Most public schools readily provide special education support or develop a plan for accommodating everything from allergies to anxiety to ADHD. Unfortunately, in their effort to provide accommodations, the child's giftedness is frequently overlooked by the school. Gifted children's academic needs are viewed as less pressing; overworked and harried teachers often provide enrichment as an afterthought. Gifted children sometimes are asked to "tutor" fellow students or read novels silently at their desks. Typically, there is little time, energy, or funding available to meet their needs.

> *Lisa and Richard were puzzled that the school was reluctant to initiate IQ testing for their clearly gifted 7-year-old son, yet seemed to "fall all over themselves" to provide services to address his dysgraphia (which affected his writing skills). The school provided occupational therapy and even adaptive writing tools as needed. While the school was exceptionally responsive to treating their son's disability, they were resistant to acknowledging his boredom in school and the need for more challenging instruction.*

Many private schools are no better. Some offer a narrow curriculum, providing few additional resources for children with special needs or for those who are gifted. Some academically rigorous private schools may offer more challenging classes; however, they often eschew the concept of giftedness and refuse to consider that some of their high achieving students still require additional academic enrichment. When you are paying for your child's education, the frustration increases as you battle against schools with little oversight.

In response to these challenges, parents of gifted children stumble upon a fast-track education of their own, as they must quickly learn about all things gifted, sort out options, and make decisions about when and how to advocate for their child. Given the roadblocks encountered in most school districts, many parents struggle for years. As noted in Chapter 1, 60.2% of participants in the Gifted Parenting Survey worry "a lot" or "always" about the quality of their child's education. In her dissertation research on parents of gifted children, Rimlinger[4] also found that parents were highly dissatisfied with their child's school. Callahan and colleagues[7] initiated a 20-year review of gifted education in the schools and reported that little had changed or improved. In another study, Purcell and Martinson[14] surveyed parents after the school's gifted education program was eliminated. Parents described the subsequent detrimental effects on their children, such as a decrease in curiosity and intrinsic motivation, and disengagement from their education. They reported that half of the parents interviewed found the school situation so untenable that they were considering alternative educational options.

This reality leaves parents scrambling for solutions. Many parents advocate with teachers, administrators, and school boards. They read books, scour the internet, and attend countless parent-teacher conferences. They investigate charter schools, cyber schools, and private schools. Some decide to scale back on their careers to homeschool their children. Many pursue a never-ending quest to find affordable, engaging extra-curricular and summer activities that live up to their hype and promise a gathering of like-minded peers. They also may feel solely responsible for guiding their child's college decisions, since many overworked school counselors lack training in identifying colleges best suited to a gifted student's needs. It's not surprising that a parent might want to take this job and shove it!

Awareness of your hesitation and fears associated with advocacy is critical. It allows you to sort through the basis for any reluctance to advocate and determine whether your hesitation is based on a clear, reasoned strategy for addressing the situation, or triggered by your personal fears. Educational advocacy can be especially difficult if you are introverted, conflict-averse, reluctant to assert your needs, or worry about how others will perceive you or your child. *Will they think I am bragging or overestimating my child's abilities? Will they think my child is weird or assume I am an overbearing mom? Will they assume I am "one of those parents"—the pushy ones teachers avoid, school boards ignore, and other parents mock?*

Requesting much-needed academic support for your child may be difficult. You might question whether you (or your child) have the right to expect a more challenging curriculum. After all, the many academically struggling children in your child's class might appear more deserving of the school's attention. You may worry that extended family or neighbors will criticize you for championing the cause. And you might doubt whether you are qualified to challenge the teacher's recommendations. Keep in mind, though, that regardless of the teacher's skills or family members' well-meaning opinions, *you know your child best*. It falls on you to advocate and educate others about giftedness. If not you, then who else will do it?

Taking on a new identity

Just as your child must adapt to a new sense of self once identified as gifted, you, too, are launched into a daunting new role—*parent of a gifted child*. Regardless of whether this role was desired or not, it has landed on your doorstep. This unexpected new role can affect how you feel about yourself and chip away at confidence in your parenting decisions. It also can create a chasm between your experience of parenting and those of other parents in your community. Hushed comments circulate within school communities, labeling parents of the gifted as pushy or hovering or insensitive to the needs of more "deserving" children. This perception of parents of the gifted is part of the stereotyping that characterizes attitudes toward gifted families. As Silverman and Golon[1] have noted, "It is ironic that parents of the gifted are often accused of 'pushing' their children when most are hanging on for dear life!" (p. 206).

> *John and Tessa wanted to ignore the obvious signs. Their son, Ethan, was quickly outpacing his classmates and complaining he was bored. They realized they should request a cognitive evaluation from the school to assess for giftedness, but they were holding back. They worried about what a gifted label would mean for their son—if he would be targeted as a nerd or even bullied. But they also had to admit that they dreaded the role of the gifted parent. They had heard gossip from other parents complaining that parents of gifted kids were just bragging or had an inflated view of their child. They wanted to fit into their community and avoid the spotlight—or worse yet, any negative stereotypes about them as a family.*

Some parents resist the presumed expectations placed upon them, feel inadequate about their role as an advocate, or feel guilty when their child possesses multiple talents while other students struggle with mastering the basics. In her research, Keirouz[15] found that parental self-concept was one of six areas of concerns parents identified when questioned about factors directly associated with their gifted child's development. Many parents understandably want a "normal" childhood for their gifted child, and feel unprepared, resentful, and scared. Given these fears and the burden of increased expectations, some reject the role entirely. They might justify this by discounting their child's giftedness or believe claims that gifted children will "do just fine" on their own[10, 16] and are smart enough to succeed without additional academic or social/emotional support. Some might try to ignore or minimize their child's abilities or how much they differ from other children their age. Some refuse to believe that their child is gifted or dismiss the construct of giftedness entirely. Their denial may be driven by a longing to normalize their family situation, avoid conflict within their community or extended family, dodge personal criticism based on others' stereotypes, or a well-intentioned desire to help their child fit in at school. Many families strongly endorse the concept of equity and fairness for every child and consider ignoring their gifted child's academic needs if this might benefit the school community. But denying your child's giftedness, delaying validation of *what they already sense is true about themselves,* or discounting their academic needs ultimately backfires. Your child eventually will question your decisions. As with any intellectual, emotional, or behavioral challenge, ignoring their needs ultimately serves no one.

Could I be gifted, too?

As parents observe their child's advanced skills and educate themselves more about giftedness, they might start to question their own smarts. Some parents already recognize their own intelligence, and in fact, may have been identified as gifted during childhood. But others are astounded to discover that their child is gifted and attribute any genetic contribution to their spouse or some distant relative. Many of these parents view themselves as somewhat intelligent—possibly hard workers, academically striving, street smart, or creative. Few would label themselves as gifted. Yet, as Tolan[17] has noted, most parents of gifted children are "gifted ex-children" themselves. "The innate qualities of mind that are found in gifted children do not disappear as the children grow up. The unusual developmental trajectory of the gifted creates an extraordinary experience of life for the individual at any age, whether or not that individual is able to achieve in ways society recognizes and values." (p. 134).

Parents of gifted children, who are likely gifted themselves, possess many of the same traits observed among gifted children[18-24]. They possess the intelligence, critical thinking skills, conscientiousness, persistence, and ability to see the big picture—all of which enhance parenting skills. They also may experience heightened sensitivity, intense emotions, acute introspection, perfectionism, and over-thinking—just like their children. Despite some of the struggles gifted adults may face, these similarities provide a window into their child's experience and ideally foster a deeper level of understanding, compassion, and attunement.

Silverman and Golon[1] highlighted the reluctance some parents feel when considering their own giftedness. They noted that given the heritability of intelligence[25,26], many were raised in families populated by gifted family members and may have trouble distinguishing what *just seemed normal* from what is nevertheless, outside the norm. Silverman and Golon commented that: "parents may begin to recognize their own abilities when they read a list of the characteristics of giftedness. But owning one's gifts is another matter. Giftedness is so frequently conflated with recognized achievement that many parents, regardless of what they have achieved, immediately dismiss the possibility that they might be gifted" (p. 213).

In their study of exceptionally gifted children conducted over 30 years ago, Silverman and Kearney[27] described the stress some parents experienced when they realized that they, too, were gifted.

> "One father, deeply moved by the testing experience, sought counseling to understand his own abilities. As a child, he had shown the same signs of extraordinary precocity as his son, and yet this had never been recognized. His gifts went unutilized. When his son was tested, he realized his own pattern of underachievement and began to set new aspirations for himself" (p. 53).

Interestingly, Silverman and Kearney noted that many of the mothers in their study refused to consider the possibility that they were gifted and attributed any heritability to their spouses. Many of the women who had not pursued a career viewed giftedness through the lens of formally recognized achievements and could not acknowledge their innate abilities. Perrone and colleagues[28] also found gender differences in a 20-year follow-up study of gifted individuals, where men were more likely than women to view themselves as having been gifted in high school or gifted as an adult. One would hope that women's openness to appreciating their talents has progressed over the past 30 years!

Raising a gifted child can evoke memories from your childhood experiences. You might recall situations in school when you were singled out for your abilities, or asked to "tutor" other kids, or were chronically bored. You may remember masking your talents to fit in once you reached middle school or struggling with pressure to achieve in high school. Many parents of gifted children hesitantly, sheepishly start to admit that yes, perhaps, they were—*and still are*—gifted, too. It makes sense, after all. The apple doesn't fall far from the tree.

On the checklist below, consider which of the following experiences fit for you:

❑ Received recognition from parents, teachers, other adults, or students about a special skill or talent

❑ Felt confusion about your abilities (e.g., why you seemed to learn more quickly than other students)

❑ Felt frustrated with other children who grasped information at a slower pace or showed no interest in your ideas

❑ Experienced teasing, rejection from peers, or bullying due to your intellectual strengths

❑ Recalled situations where a teacher singled you out to tutor other students

❑ Experienced boredom in many of your classes

❑ Felt frustrated with how the school overlooked your gifted needs

❑ Hid your abilities from peers in middle school or high school so that you would fit in

❑ Resented that the more popular or outgoing kids received more recognition for their achievements

❑ Felt frustrated with a school that overlooked your abilities because you didn't "look gifted" (e.g., due to ethnic, cultural, or gender stereotypes; a competing learning disability; shyness)

❑ Felt criticized by neighbors, extended family, teachers, or coaches to stop talking so much, or keep your ideas to yourself, or that you think too much

❑ Felt angry that your school assumed your behaviors were oppositional in nature, rather than a response to boredom (e.g., instructed you to stop fidgeting or chatting with your classmates, disciplined you for correcting your teacher's mistakes that you detected during their instruction, refused to complete assignments you viewed as pointless since you already knew the material)

❑ Developed an awareness once you were in college or the job force (or once your child was identified as gifted) that you were gifted, even though it never was identified in school

❑ Recognized your ability (when compared to your peers) to quickly grasp information, see the big picture, and understand complexity

❑ Struggled as an adult with managing your own sensitivities, intensity, overthinking, or highly active mind

❑ Struggled as an adult with difficulty finding friends or colleagues who think on the same level as you

Acknowledging your own innate giftedness can elicit unexpected emotions, and sometimes awaken long-suppressed memories. It can stoke anger toward teachers, parents, or professors who never recognized your giftedness and failed to nurture your talents and abilities. It can evoke sadness over memories of social struggles or confusion about differences you did not fully understand. It can fuel regret over roads not taken due to insecurity and self-doubt. Understanding, appreciating, and working through residual sadness or anger is essential. On a positive note, though, acknowledging untapped giftedness as an adult can be a relief and may lead to creative new challenges and even mid-life career changes.

What we know…and *don't* know from the research about parents of gifted children

Ask any parent of a gifted child about their struggles, and you may hear the same concerns. Anxiety, isolation, and frustration often top the list. Yet, minimal research has been conducted that investigates the parent's reactions and perspectives. When parents are mentioned at all, most research, opinion articles, and self-help books address the parent's impact on their gifted child…*not* their personal reactions or feelings. A Google Scholar search of the emotional and psychological adjustment among parents of gifted children uncovered only a few studies. Instead, most articles targeted the parent's perceptions of their child's adjustment or how parenting behavior affected their gifted child. In her doctoral dissertation, McDowell[29] noted the dearth of studies related to the parent's perspective and concluded: "The nature and extent of the difficulties and joys parents of gifted children face is not well understood and the voices of the parents themselves are often missing from the literature" (p. 30). Through semi-structured interviews, McDowell found that mothers of gifted children reported anxiety, stress, exhaustion, and concerns related to stigma, social isolation, and interactions with others who did not understand giftedness. Frustration was particularly strong concerning problems with the schools.

More than 35 years ago, Colangelo and Dettmann[30] summarized 20 years of research related to parents and families of gifted children. They concluded that parents of gifted children faced different problems than those experienced by other parents, including confusion about their roles at home and with the school, the belief that they lacked sufficient knowledge about giftedness, and doubts about whether they felt prepared to raise a child possessing gifted abilities. Since most of the studies addressed how parents could support their child's development rather than the parents' well-being, the reviewers called for further research into the needs of these parents.

Jolly and Matthews[1] later reviewed studies of gifted parenting conducted over a 25-year period. They noted substantial limitations and gaps in the literature and a dearth of studies overall. It was clear that Colangelo and Dettmann's call for further research focusing on parents of the gifted had not been met. Jolly and Matthews summarized what they found and classified parents' concerns across investigations into three categories: parental influence on the child, parental perception of their child's giftedness and ability, and degree of parent satisfaction with gifted programming in the schools. The parent's personal reactions, feelings, or perspectives about *being the parent of a gifted child* were not studied. In short, little research-based information is available that describes how parents cope, what level of support they need, or advice about how to handle their own heightened emotions and reactions. Rimlinger[4] also highlighted the limited amount of research addressing the effects of being the parent of a gifted child and how most studies focus on how the parent's behavior affects the child—not the reverse. She aptly noted that: "A lack of focus on the psychological well-being of parents of gifted children has resulted in limited understanding of aspects of the parents beyond basic sociodemographics" (pp. 19-20).

An early commentary on the stresses parents of gifted children face was provided by Hackney[31] over 40 years ago. Parents of gifted children participated in a discussion group and their comments were documented. Hackney described five areas of concern among the parents: their roles within the family; feeling differently about themselves; increased expectations to accommodate their gifted child's needs, such as feeling responsible for helping them reach future potential; difficulties with others' reactions to their child's giftedness, including their family and neighbors; and problems working with the school. He described parents who felt misunderstood by the community and school, were saddened by their child's difficulty fitting in with peers, felt great responsibility for ensuring that their child reached their potential, reported having made "extreme sacrifices" to accommodate their child's needs, and were burdened by feelings of guilt and fear. He noted that:

> "In some cases, parents viewed the 'gifted' label with sardonic humor. Others described their children's lives

as containing unique social and emotional qualities that produced bittersweet childhood experiences. For many families, the 'gift' often meant heavy obligation, emotional and economic drain, and in some cases, the family structure was skewed by the condition" (p. 51).

In another study, Fell and colleagues[32] compared parents of gifted children with those in the general population using the 16PF measure of personality traits. They concluded that parents of gifted children were more intelligent, independent, self-controlled, assertive, persistent, and willing to stand by their ideals. More recently, Renati and colleagues[33] identified stressors that parents of gifted children face, including advocating for improved educational services, managing their child's behavior, and difficulty obtaining support from others. The few additional available reports that specifically focus on the psychological adjustment of parents of gifted children suggest that despite their challenges and stressors, they are, nevertheless, an emotionally healthy cohort[30,34].

Given the challenges parents of gifted children face, the relative absence of research regarding the parent's well-being is striking. Rimlinger[4] pointed out that the stress of parenting children with a variety of special needs (such as children diagnosed with ADHD, ASD, developmental delays, or physical disabilities) has been studied widely. For example, she noted that a Google Scholar search targeting "autism parent well-being" revealed 26,000 results. She commented that "each diagnostic category may bring with it demands that are unique to that particular population, yet many seem to overlap and contribute to parental stress and threaten parental psychological wellbeing" (p.121). She suggested that there is commonality across conditions, such as managing daily stressors and increased demands on the family. Rimlinger's dissertation research supports her contention, as she found that parents of gifted children experience greater levels of anxiety than what is seen among the general population. This was evident even when parents of twice exceptional children were excluded from the analysis. Anxiety was most extreme among families who characterized their child's behavior as oppositional. Higher levels of parenting stress were associated with lower levels of trust toward their child's teacher, consistent with previously mentioned reports of dissatisfaction with the schools[4,7,14].

Where Do You Go From Here?

Parenting is tough. To thrive during this journey, self-awareness is essential. The more you understand about yourself, the more effectively you can parent. Self-awareness pushes you to take stock of your values and emotions and makes it more difficult to behave unconsciously or act in a manner that is counterproductive for your child. It creates an impetus to change behaviors, find another way of coping, or challenge long-standing beliefs that no longer hold true. Greater self-awareness also facilitates compassion and understanding directed toward both you and your child.

1. **Commit to developing self-acceptance and self-compassion, regardless of any discomfort with your feelings.** Everyone possesses certain "go-to" defense mechanisms. Greater awareness of how you cope when faced with troubling emotions is critical. Some parents feel so much shame about their emotions and actions that addressing them seems impossible. Others may become defensive and deny that there is any problem at all. Still others may doubt themselves and their abilities as parents. *Acceptance that frustration, regret, self-doubt, and other negative thoughts and emotions are commonplace and understandable is essential.* Shame, defensiveness, and insecurity blur the picture and make it more difficult to move beyond these feelings and behaviors.

2. **Develop a plan for educating yourself.** Learn as much as possible about gifted children as well as parenting techniques. Don't assume you can merely rely on the school to provide guidance. Reading books and articles, attending parenting workshops, and visiting online forums all provide a range of resources. Utilizing Google Scholar when searching for research-based articles can sidestep some of the pop psychology articles that may be supportive but sometimes

lack reliable information. Despite the effort required, learning more about how you can help your child, understand their development, and assess educational options should instill a greater sense of clarity and confidence.

3. **Develop a plan for self-awareness.** Start to explore the foundations for what motivates you, what worries you most, and what behaviors you want to change. Identify any thoughts, hopes, preconceived notions, expectations, family of origin beliefs, unmet personal needs, pressure from family or friends, and underlying fears that contribute to increased stress. Even more, an open awareness of how your past experiences have affected you is essential to achieving a deeper understanding of your motivations and greater clarity in your parenting decisions. As Siegel and Hartzell[3] have noted:

> *"By freeing ourselves from the constraints of our past, we can offer our children the spontaneous and connecting relationships that enable them to thrive. By deepening our ability to understand our own emotional experience, we are better able to relate empathetically with our children and promote their self-understanding and healthy development"* (p. 19).

Gaining insight into thoughts, emotions and beliefs can take some time, and a variety of self-discovery tools can be helpful. Some people benefit from a structured approach where they write down a list of their beliefs, noting what has influenced them, and then creating a plan for changing the thoughts, expectations, and beliefs that are most problematic. Others find that a more free-form approach, such as journaling or expressing themselves through art, is more enlightening. Still others find that silent meditation (or even prayer if you are so inclined), allows new ideas to flourish. Reflecting on your "personal education" through what you have learned from books, articles, workshops, or podcasts can stimulate greater understanding. Sharing your thoughts and fears with trusted family and friends, or gaining perspective from meeting with a licensed mental health professional or a member of the clergy, allows for a more personal focus on your blind spots as well as strengths.

4. **Develop a plan for supporting yourself along this parenting journey.** Identify your limits, needs, and what you can tolerate. Pace yourself, say "no" to extra demands you cannot handle, and find time for enjoyable activities. Incorporate every supportive, enjoyable, calming, and rejuvenating activity you know into your daily routine. Additionally, as the parent of a gifted child, you may require some additional support, since family and friends may not grasp why you are exhausted or stressed or frustrated. Finding a core group of like-minded parents can be invaluable. If there is a gifted parents advocacy group in your child's school district, join it. If the district lacks one, find another willing parent and start a group. You also may encounter parents through your child's extracurricular activities who understand giftedness. Online groups and forums for parents of gifted children also can provide invaluable support. (More about the benefits of support will be addressed in Chapter 4.) As mentioned above, if you feel especially anxious and distressed or if you continue to hit roadblocks with parenting, consider reaching out to a licensed mental health professional for guidance and support. Some parents resist getting help for themselves and might believe that they do not "deserve" support. Keep in mind, though, that your child will benefit from your happiness, confidence, and sense of calm. Consider it an investment in yourself that supports your entire family.

What's next?

Greater self-awareness instills clarity and confidence in your parenting decisions. It also can awaken a longing for connection with like-minded peers and parents of gifted children who are traversing this same path. You might feel isolated and misunderstood, though, and have few resources to help you along this journey. The following chapter will address the importance of camaraderie and support, along with suggestions for tracking down other adults who will truly understand.

*Any names or identifying information in clinical vignettes are disguised to protect confidentiality. Some vignettes incorporate composite descriptions as well.

CHAPTER FOUR
Finding Connection, Community, and Support

Your child is gifted—incredibly bright, curious, talented, creative, and downright amazing. So, why in the world would *you* need support? Well, for one, you might feel alone, since many of your friends and possibly most of your extended family members do not understand. You might feel overwhelmed with the responsibility of raising and educating a child whose mind is like a sponge. You might feel isolated and afraid to share your worries and concerns. You may be reluctant to tell others your child is gifted because you don't want to sound like you are bragging. Other parents who do not understand the complexities of giftedness might scoff at your concerns. They may liken parenting a gifted child to winning the lottery and find complaints unimaginable. *My child almost failed math. I wish I had your problems!* As a result, you likely keep your misgivings and frustrations to yourself.

Worries, uncertainty, and feelings of isolation are understandable and widespread among parents of gifted children. Yet, since there are few opportunities for dialogue, many parents muddle through without much guidance. Some even believe that they are alone in their ambivalence or anxiety and assume that other parents of gifted children do not experience these conflicts. Without communication or opportunities to share similar experiences, parents of gifted kids may feel just like their children do—outliers who are alone and misunderstood.

Playing by different rules

When your friends' children excel at sports or land the lead role in the school play, you readily share in their excitement. But as the parent of a gifted child, you quickly learn to play by different rules. You keep quiet about your child's accomplishments and avoid displays of emotion. You might be filled with pride, but if you share too much, you risk the appearance of bragging. If you encourage your child to excel, or sign up for an SAT prep course, you could be unjustly labeled as hovering and pushy. And if your child requires additional services at school or you advocate too vocally for the importance of gifted education, the accusations might be even worse. Elitist. Unequitable. Entitled. Selfish. The list goes on.

Parents of gifted children develop restraint, not only to avoid personal attacks but to shield their children from potential backlash. They quickly learn to soft-peddle their complaints at school, include the needs of other classroom children in requests for services, and present only cost-effective strategies to teachers and administrators that will not impose too much of a burden on staff. They also frequently downplay their child's successes. While other parents get to boast and brag, gifted parents often lurk in the background, graciously minimizing their child's accomplishments. You will not find these parents whooping and hollering at awards night; instead, they remain quietly in their seats, applauding with restraint. You won't find them announcing every Little League victory or Dean's List notification on social media. They reserve postings for only the most extreme events, like when their child wins a concerto competition or a major science research award. Even then, they often question whether sharing these accomplishments might offend other parents or create hard feelings—something parents of neurotypical children rarely consider. Do these reactions sound familiar?

Many parents of gifted children refrain from using the gifted label altogether. Researchers Matthews and colleagues[1], for example, surveyed parents of gifted children and found that most avoided using the gifted label due to concerns about eliciting negative judgments toward their children or themselves. They typically used different terms, and if their children were twice exceptional, the conversation focused more on their child's disability. If they mentioned the gifted label at all, it was used to help other parents understand giftedness as "an important aspect of individual differences" (p. 372).

When parents of gifted children finally muster up the courage to share their child's accomplishments, they frequently add an element of "undoing" into the mix. Many believe that it is immodest or impolite to discuss their child's successes so openly. If they finally choose to share, or if they receive a compliment about their child, they may feel compelled to counter or "undo" any successes with something negative. *I know she can read, but she still can't tie her shoes! Yes, he excels at math, but you should see his messy room!* Undoing is quite different from honestly confiding nagging fears to a trusted friend. It is an attempt to provide balance, reduce any inequity between your child's accomplishments and those of another child, and remove any element of discomfort from the conversation.

Playing by different rules takes its toll. It demands vigilance, a dampened spirit, and delivers a crushing blow to spontaneity. When you can't jump for joy at your child's concert, school play, math league, or award night due to fear of repercussions, your experience is diminished. You are suppressing and hiding your authentic joy over your child's successes, leaving you isolated with your strong emotions. And while you may be modeling humility and a balanced perspective for your child, you also might unintentionally convey a subdued, unenthusiastic response to some truly remarkable accomplishments.

Raising a gifted child—in a vacuum

As noted in Chapter 3, raising a gifted child ushers in an array of challenges. Parents must educate themselves about giftedness, intervene when their child struggles with social, emotional, or academic problems, and manage these tasks with little support from their community. Since giftedness (as identified by an IQ score of at least 130) comprises only 1-5% of the population, the likelihood of encountering many other families with gifted children seems slim.

Even in communities where high achievement flourishes, there still may be a limited number of parents who are raising gifted children. For example, approximately 5% of the student population were identified as gifted in the Philadelphia suburb where my children attended public school—one of three area suburban districts reporting the highest percentages. Yet, this averaged out to only one or two gifted children per classroom. Even within a community sporting a relatively high number of identified gifted children, there is limited opportunity for sharing classes with true peers. *And just as gifted students struggle to find like-minded peers, their parents also feel a similar sense of isolation.*

What happens when there are few families within your community who understand your concerns? You might feel reluctant to share your feelings, worries, and reactions. You hold back on expressing your concerns—whether related to your child's social skills, boredom in school, or even college planning—worries that might seem frivolous to other parents with different stressors of their own. Does feeling so different from others invalidate your emotions? Who can you turn to for advice, understanding, and mutual commiseration?

Navigating others' reactions

As noted in Chapter 3, your role as advocate for your gifted child comes with the territory. You find yourself clarifying, explaining, and sometimes, apologizing for your child's behavior. Most importantly, you face important decisions regarding their education, and find yourself battling educators whom you had assumed would embrace your child's love of learning. It is disturbing to discover the quiet disdain held toward gifted children and their families. It is exhausting to assert reasonable questions and even minor requests for enrichment, with little to show for it. This is particularly daunting when you are one of only a handful of parents requesting additional services. What is most puzzling is the widespread refusal to view gifted children's neurodivergent status, their learning needs, or their social/emotional struggles as worthy of time and attention. While other parents gather forces to fundraise for the Spring Fling, sponsor a book drive, or complain about too much homework, you feel like an outlier with your seemingly unique concerns. Advocating for enriched educational services is never easy, but weathering this task alone adds to the burden.

Once you start to advocate, or even casually share information about your child's abilities, some may view you differently and form assumptions. Not such nice assumptions. They may think your child is advanced in school because you pushed or hot-housed them, and spent hours with flash cards, computer programs, and private tutors. They cannot (*will not*) believe that your child needs accelerated or enriched academic programming. You become labeled as one of "them"—a pushy, short-sighted, overinvolved parent who believes their child can do no wrong. You even might be brandished as elitist, entitled, and dismissive toward struggling, at-risk students who often are portrayed as more deserving of additional educational services. These are painful accusations that no parent wants to hear. Parents of gifted children are not trying to deprive any other child—gifted, neurotypical, or at-risk—of a much-deserved education. They are trying to ensure a fair and appropriate education for their child and other gifted children whose learning needs are ignored within the classroom.

> *Sara attended a school board meeting where there was a discussion about increasing funding for gifted services. While the current programming was minimal to the point of negligence (a weekly one-hour pull-out program for elementary school students and some honors and AP courses in the high school), there was widespread resistance. One particularly unsettling comment hit hard: "Why should those gifted kids get anything more? They already have their AP courses. They have nothing to complain about." Sara was stunned by the level of bitterness among the crowd. It was clear that many of them resented gifted children and their parents—and assumed that any minor increase in gifted services would detract from what their children needed. Sara left as soon as it was over; she was afraid to run into any of these angry parents after the meeting.*

Many parents of gifted children face subtle and not-so-subtle road-blocks when it comes to helping their child. They encounter disbelief, criticism, disdain, envy, and outright challenges to what they know to be true. Some of the most common statements (i.e., myths, criticism, and unsupported assumptions) that parents of the gifted encounter include:

○ All children are gifted, each in their own special way.

○ If she is so gifted, then why doesn't she love school?

○ He will grow out of it.

○ Gifted is just high achievement—anyone can be gifted if they try hard.

○ She is already smart. She will be just fine no matter what. Why should the schools put any additional resources into her academic needs when other kids are struggling?

○ He can't be gifted if he also has ADHD.

○ She doesn't look gifted to me. I thought gifted kids were advanced, and look at how easily she cries.

○ If he's so smart, then why does he seem so immature?

○ You must have done something to get her to this point. Did you use a test-prep or grill her every night to help her get ahead?

○ Just let him be a kid! Stop pushing him with all this education stuff.

○ Gifted education is elitist.

○ You are just being a helicopter parent—just let her be a kid and stop worrying about her education.

○ Gifted education holds back other students; it creates inequity and makes other students feel inadequate.

○ If he excels in school, it must be because you pressured him.

○ I thought that kids from below the poverty line lack the resources to be gifted.

○ You will damage your child if you let her know she is gifted.

○ It's not possible that your child can excel at academics *and* music *and* sports.

○ He will do just fine at any college.

Do any of the above comments sound familiar? If not, *then just wait…*

Misinformation and assumptions based on opinions and unsupported by research dominate the conversation. Parents are left with few clear options. Do they ignore these comments and swallow their frustrations or engage in conflict to prove a point? Are they creating more problems by voicing their personal truth? Will they appear defensive or entitled? And by not defending the facts about giftedness, are they giving up on protecting their child—as well as other gifted children?

Why parents need support

The increased demands associated with raising a gifted child, adapting to your new parenting role, and gaining insight about your own history are mind-boggling. You try to stay attuned to your gifted child's social, emotional, and intellectual needs. And you are faced with a nagging sense of isolation, the sneaking suspicion that others do not get it, and reawakened memories from your own childhood about your talents. It is enough to send anyone reeling.

More than 20 years ago, Rash[2] stated the following regarding parents of gifted children: "Parents' needs have often been neglected. They frequently feel alone and confused, and they regularly receive incorrect advice from well-meaning, but ill-advised sources." (p. 14). Not much has changed since then. It is confusing and overwhelming when you must navigate a variety of opinions, criticism, harsh judgments, and a dismissive attitude toward your concerns. In fact, many parents of gifted children feel guilty about their concerns. They may subscribe to the same views as many others—that giftedness is nothing to complain about, and that they should feel lucky to have a gifted child.

Marisa felt isolated from many of her friends. They went through childbirth at roughly the same time, bonded over the travails of toddlerhood, and traded babysitting coverage on those rare "date nights" out. Yet, now she senses their discomfort as her daughter is reading at an early age, asks remarkable questions, and seems mature beyond her years. She finds herself holding back when it comes to sharing about her daughter's latest new skill and felt judged when she brought up the possibility of her daughter starting first grade early. It seems like her husband is the only person who truly gets it. Fortunately, she found out that the school district offers a gifted parents' support group. She almost cried with relief when she met other parents of gifted children who shared her feelings and offered advice for navigating the school's academic landscape. She finally could express her worries, joys, and concerns with those who truly understood.

Parents of gifted children juggle a variety of questions, expectations, demands, and parenting dilemmas that differ from what families of neurotypical children encounter. Silverman and Kearney[3], for example, studied families of exceptionally gifted children. They noted that these parents struggled with a variety of stressors, such as adjusting to the implications of IQ test results, managing their child's heightened sensitivity and intensity, identifying the best educational setting, coping with society's insensitivity toward their needs, and experiencing reactions to acknowledging their own giftedness. Some also struggled with additional financial burdens, along with the unique experience of weathering an early "empty nest," when grade acceleration prompts an earlier start date for college. In a study that assessed reactions among parents of the gifted, Renati and colleagues[4] reported that 39% felt alone or inadequate in their parenting role. Based on a review of the literature and her dissertation research, Rimmlinger[5] stressed that many gifted children should be viewed as having exceptionalities. This label would give credence to the very real struggles both gifted children and their parents face, and allow parents to voice their concerns without fear of backlash. And as one parent in the Gifted Parenting Survey commented:

"As a parent, you experience moments of intense joy, sadness, and misunderstanding. It's not easy for anyone to understand

that a 4-year-old can talk about world problems, but he cries when someone takes away his train toy…Sadly, society has a tendency to exclude the different. Anything outside the norm has a tendency to be discriminated against, bullied, or in most cases, left out."

One of the greatest concerns parents of gifted children face involves ensuring that their child receives an academically challenging education. Renati and colleagues[4] found that 50% of parents surveyed complained about the absence of support from the school. Rimmlinger[5] also found that one of the greatest identified stressors among parents stemmed from a dearth of gifted support available in the schools. Alsop[6] reported that although parents of gifted children expected to receive emotional support from the school, as well as their community, friends, and family, most were disappointed and frustrated by what they viewed as minimal support. In fact, less than 20% described their child's teacher as helpful or supportive. Alsop suggested that parents might benefit from counseling to help them address these challenges. Greenspon[7] aptly noted the experience many parents face:

> "Many of us have been viewed as 'nerds,' 'oddballs,' or elitists—that is to say, we have been othered—and have been treated accordingly. Many of us have attempted to pursue services for which our children have well-established needs but which the larger society fails to see as justified" (p. 125).

The relative absence of support, guidance, or validation can take a toll. Struggling to address your gifted or twice exceptional child's social, emotional, and academic needs in isolation can lead to feelings of distress. Some parents experience psychological symptoms, such as depression, anxiety, physical complaints, sleeplessness, increased worrying, anger, frustration, and hopelessness. Others may engage in unhealthy behaviors such as excessive alcohol use or overeating to distract them from their distress. At the very least, the absence of support can evoke feelings of bitterness, envy, and cynicism. While not all parents of gifted children experience these symptoms, many recognize they are struggling and actively seek support. They appreciate that without guidance from others who have navigated this experience, they will struggle—and perhaps, make parenting decisions they might regret. It also should be noted that persons of color often endure even greater challenges and feelings of isolation in their gifted advocacy and parenting efforts. Greenspon[7] has emphasized the importance of empathy for families affected by racism, and coined the term, "empathic resonance" to describe what is needed. He emphasized that although White individuals can never fully appreciate the experiences persons of color face, they must find "points of connection" where greater understanding is reached.

Numerous studies have pointed to the emotional and physiological benefits of social support[9-11] and its effects on parental well-being[12,13]. However, only a few studies have investigated the benefits of support for parents of gifted children[14-17]. Silverman and Golon[17] found that parents of gifted children who sought psychological support had the following goals: confirming that their child was gifted, parenting and advocacy advice, identifying appropriate educational goals, locating resources, managing family dynamics, and obtaining advice related to specific concerns, such as twice exceptional issues, underachievement, and peer relationships. They concluded the following:

> "Parents of the gifted need as much support as their children. As the primary influence in their children's lives, they should be perceived as partners in the emotional and academic development of their children. Parents have fought for provisions for the gifted and are invaluable allies in keeping special programs alive" (p. 199).

If you are not already involved in a gifted parents' support or advocacy group, it would be well worth your time to try to find (or start) one. Whether in person, through the school, or in online forums, parents can unload their fears, gain valuable advice, and enlist others in their advocacy efforts. When parents of gifted children find other adults who understand giftedness, they receive an invaluable source of support; a resource where they can gain much-needed information, personal validation and support, and potential allies in advocacy battles. They can direct you to hard-to-find resources, warn you about whom to avoid when advocating within the schools, listen empathetically to your complaints and worries, and even share recommendations about preparing your child for college. Meeting with other parents of gifted children, or with those whose children participate in a shared extra-curricular activity, is a relief and a powerful antidote to isolation.

How parenting support affects your child

Parenting research has found evidence of more successful outcomes for children (such as overall adjustment or a reduction in behavior problems) when parents receive family, social, and community support—whether for first-time parents, raising children with special needs, or when coping with the challenges of adolescence[18-22]. The added stress associated with parenting a gifted child not only can evoke strong emotions and reactions (such as hopelessness or anxiety), but those emotions can be inadvertently projected onto your child. When you are stressed, overwhelmed, and uncertain about how to proceed, your frustration can be discharged through irritability, distractibility, and harsh responses. Everyone has a bad day and can be irritable or abrupt. However, the responsibility associated with parenting a gifted child creates additional, challenging, daily stressors. In addition, life may be particularly stressful for parents of twice exceptional children. For example, studies have highlighted the additional stress families face when their child is diagnosed with ADHD[23,24] or ASD[25, 26].

> *Lauren still regrets how she acted with her oldest child when he was young. She realizes that she was impatient with his quirks and his reluctance to socialize with the other neighborhood kids. She just wanted him to be "normal" and not require so much additional support. She would snap at him and even bribe him to play with the other kids. She was worried about his emotional development and felt unable to contain herself. She realizes now that she took her anxiety out on him.*

Many researchers, counselors, theorists, and educators in the field of gifted education have highlighted the essential importance of education and support for parents of gifted children[27-32], along with specific recommendations, approaches, and evaluations of support services for families[33-39]. The parent's personality, attitudes about parenting, and perspective about giftedness also may have an impact. Research on personality theory, though, is no longer the popular topic for investigation it was 30+ years ago. However, Ruf[40] recently summarized a 17-year follow-up study of gifted children and their social, emotional, and career status as adults. One of the measures assessed the impact of their parents' personality traits. Ruf noted that:

> "It is the parental personality and viewpoint that most significantly make the difference in outcomes…When parents discover what works most naturally for their child's ways of learning, they can take positive actions to find an environment that already exists or they can establish an environment that opens up a good "fit" not only in their child's learning and academic realm, but in the social, emotional, and eventual adult career domains, as well" (p. 80).

Group support for parents of gifted children

Gifted parenting support and education are frequently delivered through support groups or workshops. Braggett and colleagues[41] described the advice parents sought from parenting workshops. They were interested in acquiring a greater understanding of the child's social/ emotional and intellectual development, expressed worries related to their child's motivation or boredom at school, were frustrated with teachers whom they perceived as threatened by the needs of gifted children, sought a comprehensive understanding of the school system, and wanted more information about enrichment activities related to their child's interests. The authors noted that "overall, they wanted reassurance that their youngsters, although gifted, were normal children" (p. 80). Free[15] also described the beneficial effects of an informal support group that arose as part of research on the psychosocial needs of parents of gifted children. "SENG Model Parent Groups"[34] provide supportive, informational groups where parents can share their concerns and learn more about their gifted child's development. Some schools provide groups or workshops for parents of gifted children as well. Local, state-based, and national organizations, such as SENG (Supporting the Emotional Needs of the Gifted), GHF (Gifted Homeschoolers Forum), and NAGC (National Association for Gifted Children) also offer conferences and online workshops for parents of gifted and twice exceptional children.

Unfortunately, there is little available research on the effectiveness of support groups for parents of gifted children. One might assume that support groups would be helpful; however, without identifying more specifics (such as the type of group, their goals and mission, how they are formed, or whether they are led by professionals or current members), statements documenting their benefits are mostly anecdotal. Those few studies targeting the impact of such groups primarily focus on how well parents were educated about giftedness and how this affected their child. For example, Weber and Stanley[39] reported that parents demonstrated an increase in their understanding of the process of gifted identification, the characteristics of gifted children, appropriate education for gifted students, and parenting practices. In another study, Morawska and Sanders[42] found that a parent's level of confidence in their parenting skills was associated with the degree of behavioral and emotional problems their child exhibited. When compared to a waitlist control group, parents who participated in a group intervention designed to improve parenting skills reported a reduction in problematic child behaviors, such as hyperactivity. They also reported significant improvements in their parenting style, with a decrease in either permissiveness or harshness when disciplining their child.

Research on the effectiveness of SENG Model Parent Groups has focused on how group parenting support has an impact on the child. DeVries and Webb[34] highlighted the importance of support for parents of gifted children, along with their implementation of groups designed to provide both education and support. As they noted, "Parents of gifted children experience an unsettling dissonance between the child-rearing practices recommended for average children and the reality of the child in their midst" (p.3). SENG Model Parent Groups attempt to address this disparity. DeVries and Webb claimed that through the parent's enhanced understanding of the needs of gifted children, potential emotional or behavioral problems that might arise can be thwarted. While these groups likely increase confidence and clarity in parenting decisions, they are not specifically focused on the parent's well-being; like many programs, they target improvement in parenting skills. Saranli and Metin[38] studied SENG Model Parent Groups and reported that parents felt their ability to support their gifted child had improved, although the children interviewed did not identify any change in their perception of support received from parents.

In her dissertation research, Adler[33] failed to identify a significant difference on outcome measures when comparing group support for families of gifted children with a control group. Nevertheless, she highlighted subjective comments voiced by families of gifted children who participated in the support group, which she claimed documented their positive impact:

> "One of the main issues that parents brought up was find-
> ing other parents who went through similar experiences.
> Some representative comments follow: 'I was greatly
> relieved to hear about other people's children who sounded
> like mine. I had previously felt like an alien.' 'It was great
> to be able to interact with other parents who have similar
> issues.' 'I realized I was not alone in having difficulties
> in understanding and dealing with my child.' 'Prior to
> attending this support group, I/we felt alone, isolated,
> fearful, mistreated, etc. The information I received, the
> knowledge I have gained, very well may have prevented a
> break-down'" (p 118).

Parenting is hard enough. Parenting a gifted or twice exceptional child complicates the task and ushers in a range of stressors, demands, and reactions. It makes sense that without guidance and support, it becomes much more difficult to understand, manage, and contain your emotions. Without support, any lingering fears, frustrations, and disappointments may be projected onto your child. Despite the shortage of research on the effectiveness of group support for parents of gifted children, it is still likely that such groups are quite helpful, especially given the proven benefits accrued from group support research for so many other conditions. As a psychologist, I have witnessed the powerful, positive effects that can be achieved through group participation. These include a shared sense of mission and purpose, camaraderie, guidance from others who truly understand, a renewed sense of hope when witnessing others' success with overcoming similar problems, and gentle confrontation when needed. What is most important when searching for a group is finding the right fit, where you can join parents with common goals and experiences.

How do you find support?

Social support, self-awareness, and a willingness to embrace and learn from the gifted parenting role are critical to increasing your confidence, joy, and satisfaction as a parent—and to the well-being of your child. It is a much-welcomed relief to find other adults who truly understand your experience and can provide support and encouragement. In addition to those family and friends who "get it," reaching out to other parents of gifted children is essential, whether through your neighborhood, at your child's school, or through online forums and groups. Gifted parent advocacy groups exist in many school districts and provide both a venue for support and idea exchange, but also a vehicle for initiating change within the district. School administrators are typically more receptive to recommendations from parent groups than from one individual alone, and any potential changes that follow will impact many children—not just your own child. The following are a few steps to consider:

1. **Gather as much information as possible through exploration of available resources.** Read books about gifted children, gifted education, and any relevant twice exceptional conditions that pertain to your child, such as ADHD or a learning disability. A variety of excellent books[27-32] about parenting gifted children are available, with most highlighting information similar to the conclusions Matthews and colleagues[1] noted above. Although this task may seem daunting, the more information you obtain, the more you

can wisely challenge school recommendations, counter misinformation about giftedness, and most importantly, understand your child's social, emotional, and academic needs. Your confidence as a parent and advocate for your child will improve.

Scour the internet for relevant, research-based information. At the time of this writing, the most widely used website sources include the National Association for Gifted Children (NAGC), Supporting the Emotional Needs of the Gifted (SENG), Gifted Homeschooler's Forum (GHF), Hoagie's Gifted Education Page, and The Davidson Institute. Use Google Scholar when searching for the latest research. Attend webinars provided online, along with in-person workshops through your school district, local gifted parenting groups, or state-based gifted education organizations. Use some caution when relying on personal anecdotes and advice, though. Some social media sites include comments from well-meaning parents who offer very directive advice. While it can be validating to hear from other parents who have been down this road before, what worked for them may not necessarily help your family. Information and advice you receive should be kept in perspective.

2. **Join a group for parents of gifted children.** Locate a pre-existing group within your community, school district, homeschooling cooperative, or even within an extra-curricular activity your child frequents. As noted earlier in this chapter, group support enhances self-awareness, confidence, and understanding of the social, emotional, and academic challenges your child faces. In addition to the personal support derived from connections formed with like-minded families, many groups share a common goal or mission, and members work together to effect meaningful changes within the schools. In some school districts, parent advocacy groups are welcomed, and parents are enlisted to work alongside teachers and administrators to challenge

social policy, attend and provide support during individualized education planning meetings, and demand changes in how gifted services are implemented. Like in many organizations, sometimes "outsiders" (in this case, parents who do not work for the school) have little to lose when challenging the system; their jobs are not on the line, and they can advocate without fear of repercussions.

If you cannot find a gifted parenting support group in your area, you can start one. Depending on the group's goals, this might consist of an informal gathering of parents or a more formalized program through your school district. Ask the gifted support supervisor at your school to share information about the proposed group with other parents; if your school lacks any gifted programming, you might check with the school psychologist, guidance counselor, or principal. The group could be free-standing or set up as an affiliate with your state-based gifted education organization, if one exists. Here in Pennsylvania, for example, many school districts have affiliate groups associated with the Pennsylvania Association for Gifted Education (PAGE). If you homeschool your child, you might form a group that includes parents from a local homeschooling cooperative. The NAGC has provided helpful suggestions for starting a gifted parents group, with useful tips for defining goals, a mission, and guidelines for sustaining the group.[36, 43]. Nilles[36] has suggested that given the many directions parenting groups can take, participants should establish their purpose, mission. and goals. Some of the groups Nilles highlights are specifically geared toward parents; others include activities for families and their children that engage the children's interests.

3. **Find support online.** While locally based, in-person support is ideal, some online groups and forums for parents of gifted children can supplement local resources or provide information and support when local options are unavailable. Online sites, such as those found on social media or on sites such as GHF or The Davidson Institute, provide advice, support,

and information shared by other parents who often understand your struggles. As one parent in the Gifted Parenting Survey noted:

> *"It's very isolating when your 18-month-old has 1000 words and all of my friends' kids of the same age barely communicate. It was almost scary how different she was from her peers. I felt like we were navigating it alone until finding the right books and online communities with other parents in the same situation."*

While the support you may obtain from online groups can be validating, please use discretion when sharing information that could inadvertently create problems for your child later in life. You may discover that some parents, eager to obtain information and support, share highly personal information online about their child, ranging from IQ scores to struggles with drug addiction or clinical depression. Once that information is available online, it can be accessed by anyone—college admissions officers, future employers, and even law enforcement agencies. If what you feel compelled to share might be incriminating, please use restraint and express your worries and concerns more directly with family, friends, or professionals you trust.

4. **Embrace self-care.** It would be an oversight to ignore the essential benefits associated with self-care. Unfortunately, this term sometimes evokes a negative reaction, and an assumption that a demanding regimen of personal discipline and lifestyle changes are required. Yes, self-care encompasses various "maintenance" functions that we all strive to achieve, such as a balanced diet, good sleep hygiene, regular exercise, and a calming relaxation practice, such as meditation. But it also includes joyful, creative, relational activities—spending time with beloved family and friends, engaging in relaxing hobbies, finding outlets that provide joy and meaning, and taking time to have fun. Self-care might include personal

time for you (such as reading, a creative hobby, watching film and TV, or walking in nature) or time with others (such as conversing with trusted friends, "date night" with a partner or spouse, or playing games with your children).

Enlisting the services of other professionals if needed and if affordable may be a part of self-care as well—guidance from a meditation teacher; body work with a massage therapist, acupuncturist, chiropractor, or physical therapist; exercise with a personal trainer; or even using a meal delivery service. Some find spiritual devotion essential. Others immerse themselves in a daily dose of time spent outdoors. Self-care can be considered a philosophy that honors your limits, energy level, and personal needs. Limiting obligations, saying "no" when necessary, pacing yourself, and taking breaks to relax throughout the day are essential. Ultimately, if you take care of your own needs and feel happy, rested, energized, and confident, you can more readily meet the needs of your children.

5. **Seek professional support.** This includes support for your child when needed, as well as for yourself. When you have concerns about your child's academic or emotional well-being, seek support. Ask questions and gather information from a trusted teacher, gifted support supervisor, pediatrician, school psychologist, school counselor or licensed mental health professional familiar with issues associated with giftedness. These professionals can provide guidance tailored specifically to your child's unique needs. They will take your child's strengths and challenges into account, along with your family's needs, and recommend available local resources. Mental health professionals, in particular, are trained to respond to specific parenting questions, such as when to push your child and when to hold back. They also can assess your child's social and emotional well-being, and offer guidance related to asynchronous development, social immaturity, emotional reactivity, perfectionism, and underachievement. They can guide you through any challenges in

terms of family dynamics (such as marital conflicts related to child-raising or how to address caring grandparents who challenge your parenting decisions) and help with academic decisions (such as the benefits and drawbacks of full grade acceleration or whether to encourage a gap year after high school). Your child does not need a mental health diagnosis to benefit from support; do not hesitate to reach out if needed. Of course, *if your child exhibits signs of emotional distress, such as depression, anxiety, behavioral problems, addictive behaviors, or evidence of self-harm or suicidal thinking, it is essential to address these problems immediately with a mental health professional.*

Consider your own needs as well. Parents get stressed; it comes with the territory. When self-help strategies fail, or when the stress becomes overwhelming, seeking support from a trusted professional is beneficial. Some people also prefer the personalized focus and confidentiality obtained through individual counseling, particularly if they are reluctant to share information within parenting support groups. Some concerns also require more professional expertise and individualized attention than what can be found within an educational or support group format. Clear symptoms that warrant further support include (but are not limited to): feelings of hopelessness, despair, unresolved grief, excessive anxiety, obsessive worrying, a change in eating or sleeping patterns, intense anger, or physical complaints associated with your distress. Family crises and personal losses, such as divorce, death of a loved one, job stress, health problems, caring for an elderly family member, excessive problematic behaviors (alcohol or substance abuse, eating disordered symptoms, overworking, overexercising, or overspending), or marital distress may signal the need for support. Of course, suicidal thoughts, self-harm, or an environment where domestic violence is present call for immediate action. If your primary care physician or psychotherapist are not available and you are in crisis, contacting a local crisis line or your hospital emergency department is essential.

Serious mental health needs are not the only reason people seek psychotherapy, though. You don't have to be miserable to consider this path toward greater self-awareness and understanding. Many people benefit from exploring their thoughts, feelings, or unwanted behaviors, and finding solutions in collaboration with a skilled psychotherapist. While it is ideal to find a therapist who has experience with gifted individuals and families, this niche is highly specialized, so you may have difficulty finding a therapist who meets this criterion. And often, a "specialist" is not necessary; many highly skilled therapists can understand your presenting concerns and provide valuable assistance, even without a framework that includes information related to giftedness.

Here are some guidelines to consider when searching for a mental health professional. Start by checking for referrals from your primary care physician or nurse practitioner, school psychologist, guidance counselors at your child's school, faith-based organization, or even from family or friends. Review a list of therapists who specialize in giftedness on sites such as Hoagie's Gifted Education Page or SENG, as well as listings through your state-based gifted education association. Check with local and state-based mental health professional associations for referrals. If you want to address a specific problem, such as anxiety, depression, substance abuse or an eating disorder, you could check with national organizations dedicated to providing information and resources related to these concerns. Keep in mind that even if a therapist is highly recommended by a trusted professional, that therapist may not be the best fit for you. So, shop around to find someone whom you will trust.

What's next?

In the next few chapters, specific emotions that parents of gifted children commonly experience will be addressed, along with how your reactions might affect your child. The more you understand your personal reactions related to your child's giftedness, the more likely you will feel confident, clear, and equipped to manage any challenges that may arise.

Chapter Five
The Sky Is the Limit—Pride, Joy, and High Expectations

You love your child completely, and you know that accomplishments aren't everything. Yet sometimes you feel like you might burst with pride, especially when your gifted child achieves something extraordinary. You feel it when they reach milestones at a remarkably early age, achieve outstanding success in a particular activity, or express unusual insight about the complexity of the world. You are in awe of their abilities, talent, and precocious behavior, and slightly stunned that you have such an amazing child. But you sometimes might feel guilty, since giftedness is not a choice, and you know you would love your child regardless of their talents.

Just like parents of neurotypical children, you feel pride and excitement over your child's achievements even when they are not particularly dramatic—landing a role in the school play, overcoming hurdles in a challenging subject, or scoring the winning soccer goal. But other times, their accomplishments are quite spectacular, driven by your gifted child's boundless curiosity, or sheer effort to master something meaningful, or passionate immersion in a beloved interest. These are the very young children who categorize every known dinosaur, who practice an instrument for hours, who build intricate LEGO structures, or devour chapter books once they start to read. These are the elementary school-aged children who join ballet companies, or win chess tournaments, or write letters to their congressperson demanding assistance for the homeless. These are the teens who win concerto competitions, who excel at advanced college math courses, or win awards for innovative science fair projects.

Sometimes you have something to brag about…but can't. Your child might accomplish something truly amazing, and you have no one to share this with. You don't want to boast. You don't want to seem like you are exaggerating. You don't want to "bore" your friends with yet another story of your child's success. Other parents broadcast their child's accomplishments (*My son made honor roll this semester. My daughter will be in the school play*). But there may be little room to mention, for example, that your son *always* gets straight A's, or that your daughter consistently has the lead in both the school play and community theater. Unless you are speaking with other parents of gifted children, or with family and friends who truly understand, it may be difficult to honestly share your child's strengths without triggering discomfort, envy, or even disbelief. You learn to keep it to yourself.

> *Jenny was sitting with parents at the PTA, who were complaining about how hard all the honors and AP classes were, and how kids only take these classes because their parents push them. Yet, Jenny kept thinking about what a relief it was for her son to have these classes, and how he finally felt challenged for the first time. He was excelling, and in fact, these classes were still fairly easy for him. But Jenny felt she couldn't challenge the other parents' views because it might seem like bragging. So, she just nodded and kept her thoughts to herself.*

Most parents of gifted children are *just along for the ride* and trying to keep up with their child's intensity. They have no interest in prepping or pushing their child to excel. But parents of neurotypical children—your neighbors, extended family, fellow parents at your child's school—may not understand. Their skepticism is palpable, and they may suspect that you have spent hours coaching or pressuring your child to succeed. And you worry that they view you as overly involved; bragging or exaggerating your child's accomplishments. One parent in the Gifted Parenting Survey described several of the dilemmas parents face when unable to share their excitement or advocate for their child:

> *"That parents of neurotypical children think you are overreacting when seeking help for your gifted child. Feeling like you cannot celebrate any successes because nobody wants to hear, because it makes them feel a failure as a parent because their child cannot do x, y, or z. Having defensive teachers who don't believe that the student is in fact gifted. Being thought of as a pushy parent. Having no other parent friends who have gifted kids (no tribe to understand). All the while reveling in and being frustrated by this beautiful little mind."*

Despite some of the challenges parents of gifted children face, most are thrilled with their child and amazed at their talents. Many are grateful and appreciative of their child's sensitivity, compassion for others, and their ability to excel academically. Their thirst for knowledge, their curiosity, and their passion for what interests them is a sight to behold. In fact, most participants (90.1%) in the Gifted Parenting Survey reported "often" or "always" feeling grateful that their child is so creative, intellectually curious, sensitive, or empathetic. Over half of the parents also indicated that they "often" or "always" feel grateful that their child excels in and enjoys school (52.2%). This suggests that even within this sample where concerns regarding emotional and social adjustment or school limitations were evident, the majority of parents felt gratitude and appreciation for their child's intensity and intellectual capabilities.

Many parents of gifted children resent accusations that they are pushy and overinvolved, and recoil from labels like "stage mom" or the "tiger mom" characterization in Amu Chua's[1] memoir about raising her talented children. In a remarkable *parallel process*, just as your child may be downplaying their giftedness to fit in with peers, you also may be learning to suppress and modulate your joy and excitement in the presence of other adults. Instead of a spontaneous expression of joy, you might weigh and measure the appropriateness of your reactions. *I won't applaud too loudly at the concert because other parents might think*

I'm boasting. I won't tell my friends about her recent award because she's already won three others, and they might start to resent it. You quickly recognize the futility of sharing your excitement with adults who misinterpret your motives, or even worse, gossip and criticize.

> *Mike remembers a middle school talent show. There were karaoke performances and pop songs that received whoops and hollers from the audience. Some parents even brought bouquets for their children. But when his daughter got up there and performed a highly advanced cello sonata, many of the kids in the audience got bored and started talking while she was playing. He overheard a parent behind him comment that "hey, she's really good," but after she was done, there was only polite applause. No shouts. No acclaim. She looked so vulnerable and alone up there, quickly bowing after the performance and leaving the stage as soon as possible. He thought she knew she did a good job, but felt saddened to see how much she differed from the other kids. And he realized that he didn't fit in with most of the other families either.*

Of course, some might say that they *wish* they had this "problem"—raising a child capable of remarkable accomplishments, even if they feel compelled to restrain themselves from sharing their joy. But there are repercussions when you consistently press the mute button and suppress enthusiasm about your child. For one, your child may receive mixed signals. They may notice other parents showing excitement over seemingly minor achievements, while you only react to their most stellar accomplishments. Your child might be puzzled about your stunted enthusiasm and interpret this as a signal that they always must excel or assume that more routine accomplishments are meaningless. They may develop a distorted sense of what is expected of them and assume a hefty burden due to their talents. They also might feel guilty about their own achievements, toning down any sense of pride when they succeed. Given enough time, they might rebel completely through underachieving or abandoning a once beloved talent.

Why is it important to acknowledge your child's success?

Most parents experience pride, excitement and even relief when their child reaches developmental milestones, such as their baby's first steps or their first few words. That first report card or ballet recital or hockey game can be hallmark events. It is entirely normal to feel excited about your child's accomplishments—and to show your child how much you care. Psychotherapy theorists and researchers[2-4] have noted the importance of attunement for babies and toddlers; young children need to feel that their parents understand and adore them— that they are attuned to their moods and needs. The parent's "twinkle in the eye" is an essential source of recognition and encouragement. Infants who have been deprived of a sense of attunement from their caregivers, such as when there is tremendous loss within the family, or if they are placed in understaffed facilities awaiting adoption, often suffer from attachment anxiety or heightened responsivity to stress[5,6].

However, perfection is never expected! In fact, Winnicott's[7] classic description of the "good enough" caretaker emphasizes the normal and necessary progression from when the parent is ever-present, to when the child must tolerate minor frustrations. This experience builds trust and resilience, as the child still feels loved and understood, recognizes that the parent is not always readily available, but feels confident that the loving parent will return. They learn to forge ahead with the confidence that their newfound adventures are encouraged, but also know there is a safety net of love and appreciation. Children are quite resilient and accept that parents can be irritable or make mistakes or get distracted. They may not like it, but recognize that the foundation of love and acceptance is still there.

The challenge that falls on you as a parent can be daunting. Learning how, when, and how much to encourage your gifted child is essential. They need your praise and attention—but tempered with clarity about what is praise-worthy. Gifted children can sniff out false praise. Just as most children realize that their soccer team's trophy (*just for finishing the season*) means very little, your child may discount compliments if they are not tethered to an actual achievement. Lavish praise for completing every homework assignment or household chore, though, will be viewed with suspicion, or at least disrespect regarding your judgment. A simple "thank you" is sufficient and much appreciated. Most importantly, they need to know that you love them for who they are—regardless of their mistakes, failures, or accomplishments. The following questions for self-reflection may be useful:

> *How do I feel about enthusiastic displays of emotion in general? Am I comfortable showing others how I feel or how much I care? Have I been criticized in the past for showing too much emotion—or, conversely, not enough emotion? How did my family of origin react to outward displays of enthusiasm?*

> *What are my opinions about communicating to others about my child's accomplishments? Do I feel that I should tone things down, or is it good to share successes with friends and family? Do I feel excited for others who share their child's or their own accomplishments, or do I sometimes cringe when it seems excessive? How did my family of origin react to my achievements?*

> *Do I feel a little guilty that my child is blessed with such strong abilities when other parents comment about their child's academic troubles? Since my child is so fortunate to possess these gifts, do I have the right to broadcast these accomplishments?*

Understanding your own personal reactions to your child's achievements and how these influence your enthusiasm is essential. Greater awareness will free you from the bonds stemming your own childhood or family influences, along with inhibitions related to concerns about what others might think. The more you are aware of how these emotions and beliefs affect your behavior, the more you can achieve clarity and confidence over how you respond to your child's abilities. You are entitled to experience feelings of pride, joy, and astonishment as you observe your child's flourishing abilities. Sharing your feelings with a select group of supportive, understanding adults (as noted in Chapter 4) can enhance your sense of well-being. The following are some guidelines to consider:

1. **Continue to show your child how much you enjoy their openness, warmth, and humor, and convey that you love spending time with them.** Your love for them is not tied to their behavior or accomplishments. Yes, you can express your displeasure when they misbehave, and express joy and excitement over their achievements. But they need to know that your love is unconditional.

2. **Comment on their progress rather than merely the finished product.** Let them know that you recognize their efforts and are proud of their hard work. Comment about how most difficult achievements take struggle and effort, and you value their dedication even more than the outcome.

3. **Help them grapple with any confusion and possibly some ambivalence about their exceptional talent.** Let them know that you recognize their abilities, and that it engenders potential that they can mold as they progress through school and career. It will be their choice to decide what they will do with their talents, but you will support them by offering guidance and feedback along the way. Treat their giftedness as just one aspect of who they are, but one where they have choices about how to use their abilities.

4. **Encourage them to take appropriate social risks.** Inviting a friend over to play, attending a party, or going to the dance can be challenging, especially when the possibility of rejection looms large. Help them also appreciate that their neurotypical friends have amazing traits as well. They don't need to stop themselves from excelling just to fit in; however, they can learn to be humble and pick the right time and place to display their strengths. Offer praise when you notice their patience, humility, kindness, and tolerance, as well as when they stand up to peer pressure and refuse to conform to inappropriate social expectations.

5. **Share your excitement over progress in areas that are difficult for them.** Cheer for them especially when tackling an activity where they typically do not excel; show enthusiasm over an art project, their commitment to the track team, or their B in math. Let them know how much you value their hard work or collaborative team spirit—even when they do not excel in these activities.

6. **Have a frank conversation with them about their giftedness.** Ask them in a matter-of-fact manner how they feel about possessing certain strengths, along with areas of difficulty. Just as they may delve into a fascinating science project, or shine in creative writing, they also may struggle with disorganization, procrastination, or a reluctance to take on new and challenging tasks. Speak about these observations as behaviors that can be addressed—opportunities to grasp or problems to solve.

The conundrum of high expectations

Children need to know that we expect them to succeed and believe in their abilities. Regardless of whether expectations include developmentally appropriate tasks or chores, or if they are associated with gifted abilities and talents, children learn important life lessons when we impart reasonable expectations. These might be as mundane as keeping their room clean, showing respect for others' belongings, learning to control their temper, or getting to school on time. Children benefit from both love and limits; in fact, an absence of structure, limits, and reasonably appropriate expectations can backfire. (More about this will be addressed in Ch. 8.)

Maintaining positive, realistic, and appropriately high expectations for your child lays the groundwork for their own path toward internalizing values related to responsibility and achievement. They realize that a responsible adherence to family, social, and cultural values allows them to function within our society. It boosts their self-esteem when they complete tasks and behave responsibly. When families, schools, and society at large encourage children to excel, yet also provide loving encouragement to overcome roadblocks and rebound from failure, they learn to accept a process toward future personal growth. Gifted children quickly realize that *their* tasks and responsibilities may differ from those of their peers. Easy A's in school may be fun at first, but seem empty after a while. They recognize that their trajectory toward success is a rewarding path that will unfold if they push themselves to meet these expectations.

As parents, we are called upon not only to hold appropriately high expectations for our children, but also to create room for failure and disappointments through a (sometimes) haphazard journey toward achieving their goals. Accomplishments need to be considered from a variety of perspectives. Success might involve excelling at a high level in an area of talent; it also can mean adopting organizational skills, overcoming social anxiety, staying focused in a class they dislike, or showing kindness toward those less fortunate. Identifying what to expect from your child will require attunement to their abilities, skills, interests, developmental level, emotional temperament, frustration tolerance, and the social climate where they attend school. Quite a lot to juggle! But, as mentioned before, you don't have to be perfect, and you always can increase, lower, or change your expectations.

Sandra and Jeff recognized their daughter, Katie's love of theater and imaginary play from an early age. Once oppor-tunities arose in school, she quickly jumped at the chance. Katie typically landed the lead role and loved acting. When further opportunities for children's roles in community theatre became available, they encouraged her to audition. Although she was accepted, she was given a small part, and essentially remained in the background. After the performance, she felt disappointed and disillusioned. She preferred the excitement of the plays at school where she was a star. She wanted to drop out of community theater, even though it would be a much more challenging place to hone her skills. Sandra and Jeff struggled with how to react. Should they encourage her to remain in community theater and learn to tolerate the expectations and disappointments that are part of a more demanding venue?

Or should they allow her "to be a kid" and stick with the less challenging roles at school?

Ultimately, gifted children (like everyone else) will hit a roadblock along the way. For a child who always excels or who assumes that all learning should be fun, the fallout can feel devastating. They are used to success and cannot imagine that they might fail. Helping your child build resilience, or the ability to bounce back from setbacks, is an essential life skill. Keeping expectations high but supporting your child through the normal disappointments they encounter is part of parenting. Sometimes setbacks occur when a more demanding challenge is introduced. Like Katie in the vignette above, many children reach a point where academic, athletic, or artistic challenges require greater effort, maturity, and a willingness to (at least temporarily) let go of their assumption that they will be the star, or that they are immune to setbacks.

Underachievement plagues many gifted children, teens, and adults[8,9]. Even when parents maintain appropriately high expectations, the norms within their school, social, and cultural worlds take their toll and can dampen their enthusiasm. When gifted children can coast through school with little effort, they may develop a false sense of confidence. Social pressure to hide their giftedness, boredom in school, disillusionment with authority figures, and an absence of self-regulation skills (such as time management and organizational skills) may lead to a crash landing. When they eventually hit roadblocks—a class or job that is difficult or demanding—they experience a harsh awakening. The stunning awareness that sole reliance on their natural talents is insufficient can shake their sense of self and result in shame and profound self-doubt. It also may lead them to avoid any difficult task in the future. They had equated giftedness with automatic learning and are shocked and devastated when they see that they also must work hard to achieve. As I have commented elsewhere about gifted underachievement: "Coasting through school can contribute to a distorted perspective about the extent of one's talents, and an expectation that any task should be easy…Some people are able to put a challenge or failure experience into perspective more easily than others, but if confronting failure has never been within a student's repertoire, hitting a roadblock can be devastating" [10] (p. 142).

Inman[11] has described what children fail to learn when they are never challenged. They are denied an opportunity to develop a sense of responsibility, decision-making and problem-solving skills, a strong work ethic, the strength to cope with failure, the self-worth derived from accomplishments, and a capacity for sacrifice. In essence, gifted children not only fail to acquire essential self-regulation skills but are deprived of "character-building" opportunities. Accomplishments mean little because they come too easily, and they miss out on learning the importance of hard work, sacrifice, "paying your dues," and surmounting obstacles. As Inman summarized: "So, what does a child not learn when he earns good grades and high praise without having to make much effort? Simply put, he doesn't learn the values and skills needed to be a productive, caring person who contributes positively to our world" (p. 17).

Gifted children engage their love of learning from an early age. They learn best when they are inspired, intrinsically motivated, and challenged by what they are learning. Researchers have emphasized the importance of helping gifted students discover what motivates them[12-14]. Ideally, they will find their passion and feel committed to pursuing challenging goals, but also remain open to accepting some tedium or personal setbacks along the way. A problem arises, though, when they assume that all learning *should* be fun. Most people do not relish memorizing multiplication tables or studying for their driver's permit. Yet, these are tasks we all endure. Gifted children and teens may complain about what they believe are pointless demands on their time, and adamantly try to convince you, their teachers, and any authority figure within earshot why they don't need to complete these tasks. Yet, personal development is enhanced through hard work and even failure[15]. Gifted students ultimately grow by exerting effort and tackling what they view as rote, boring tasks—whether through studying, dedicated practice, or physically challenging demands. Many gifted students need to *buy in* to the value of expending effort when tasks create little intrinsic joy. McCoach and Siegle[13] found that when students could not identify any value in an identified academic goal, they became unmotivated and refused to exert any effort. In research with verbally gifted students, Redding[16] emphasized the importance of helping them understand the rationale for sticking with boring, detail-oriented tasks. If they appreciate the association between their efforts and outcomes, they will find a reason to exert themselves.

Instilling appropriately high expectations is essential to preventing inertia and underachievement. The challenge for you as a parent, though, involves recognizing whether expectations are appropriate to your child's developmental level, emotional functioning, and academic abilities at any given time. How do you decide, for example, whether to insist that your child complete a routine class project, or back off and allow them to either fail or coast along with little effort? New situations and decisions arise every day, whether associated with small, routine tasks (taking out the trash), family rules (turning off electronics by 10:00 PM), or expending effort based on their potential (completing a challenging science fair project). How do you determine if you are pushing too hard…or not enough?

Managing expectations

All parents hold basic expectations for their children. These might include connection and loyalty to family, truthfulness, a modicum of respect toward adults, and following basic rules such as completing their chores. Some families have more specific expectations, such as attending religious services, caring for elderly relatives, or babysitting younger siblings. Sometimes, expectations are based on potential benefits to the child, as well as what is expedient for the family. For example, children may gain confidence and athletic skill at summer camp, which also serves as childcare for working parents. Other times, expectations reflect what parents believe will enhance their child's development, such as participation in volunteer work, art classes, competitive sports, or spending time outdoors. Providing encouragement, limit-setting, and guidance is an essential part of parenting, particularly when your child is struggling. Children learn from experience and build resilience when they feel challenged and have the freedom to fail and recover. Almost all children fall behind at something, whether it is math, meeting deadlines, or cleaning their room. When you create an expectation that your child should accomplish something they are clearly capable of achieving, you convey respect for their abilities and potential. However, when the bar is set too high, or when failure is not an option, a child may feel pressured to perform beyond their abilities.

Tremendous potential can be daunting. It can feel like you are guiding something precious and must insure its safe passage. But how do you find that precarious balance between offering encouragement and applying too much pressure? While a few parents may feel confident in their decisions, most wrestle with these questions. Will your expectations overwhelm your child, fuel resistance and rebellion, or worse yet, create anxiety, self-loathing, and insecurity? Should you discourage their participation in demanding competitions (such as sports, dance, music, chess, or science fairs) to protect them from feeling pressured? On the other hand, is it better to take their talents seriously and insist on dedicated practice, disciplined scholarship, and achieving at the highest level? Which choice will enhance your child's confidence, emotional well-being, talent development, *and* future success? The prospect of potential regret looms large.

In addition to discovering what best supports your child's intellectual, developmental, and emotional needs, you also must remain aware of your personal motivations and reactions, tempered by your values, family of origin influences, and expectations from those around you. Sometimes, our parenting decisions are consciously or unconsciously influenced by past experiences. Parents who were pressured to succeed when they were young, for example, might refrain from encouraging their gifted child to excel—fearful that they may recreate a troubling childhood experience. On the other hand, some parents become overly involved. As hard as it might be to admit, it is important to consider whether your child's accomplishments fulfill some emptiness within you, distract you from something that is missing in your life, or complete a longing you had as a child. This is especially common when a parent may have forgone a career or did not pursue their own talents. It can feel like a parent's last chance to undo a missed opportunity or a perceived mistake.

> *Jonathan was raised in an impoverished area of a large city. He knew his parents struggled to support the family. His keen intellect was not a concern for his family; they were proud of his good grades in school, but more focused on just maintaining their household. As immigrants, they also had little knowledge of the school system and trusted that the education he was receiving was sufficient. Jonathan kept a low profile at school and did not let on to other kids that he was smart. Surviving in a tough section of the city was hard enough; he didn't need a target on has back because of his intelligence. When he graduated from high school, he started working, and then eventually went to night school to complete his college degree. Now that he is financially comfortable, he wants all the best for his children. He is aware of their gifted abilities and does not want their potential squandered. He understands that his parents did not have the time or energy to support his interests, but does not want to repeat this with his children. Sometimes they complain that he is pushing them too hard, or that they just want time at home to play rather than attend so many enrichment activities. His wife also tells him to back off. But he feels compelled to push them so they will have opportunities that he never had.*

The following are some questions to consider as you examine your expectations. You might consider writing them down and elaborating on them as they relate to your personal experiences and your child's needs at different developmental stages.

- ○ What are some core expectations I hold for my child?
- ○ What do I expect from myself as a parent?
- ○ What is my role in motivating and influencing my child's accomplishments?

- How much independence should I give my child in planning for their future?

- How do I support my child to succeed?

- How have my expectations for my child changed over time as they have matured?

- What has influenced these changes in my expectations?

- How much are my expectations based on my own hopes and dreams, or influences from family or friends?

- How do experiences from childhood influence my values and parenting decisions?

- Which values and assumptions from my childhood are helpful to maintain and which are not?

Consider the above questions for personal reflection and greater self-awareness into your own motivations. These questions are not meant to criticize or scold; the more we know about our needs, wishes, expectations and fears, the more we can gain clarity and use sound judgment in our parenting decisions.

Are you too involved?

Sometimes, parents become too emotionally attached to their child's accomplishments. We have all heard of the stereotypical "stage mom" who devotes her life to her child's interests, or the parent who basks in their child's fame. Some parents are so entranced by their child's remarkable talent that they lose themselves…and lose perspective on their child's overall well-being. Talents and abilities take precedence and other needs are secondary.

Occasionally, parents may feel compelled to quit their jobs or move across the country so their child can train with a renowned athletic coach or performing arts teacher. Some move to a community with access to an academically rigorous school. Clearly, such decisions are initiated out of love and the best of intentions—sometimes with dramatic results to show for it. But these choices can be a disruption for the family. Financial hardship, frustration, and resentment among siblings can occur. Many families feel trapped and torn, with no good answer. *Should we maintain our current lifestyle and home, or move so our child has a once-in-a-lifetime opportunity to develop their talents? Will we regret either decision? And how will so much attention on one child affect our other children?*

Exceptional measures enlisted to ensure opportunities for a highly talented child can impose an emotional toll. While some children thrive when there is strong support to reach their goals, others buckle under the pressure. Sensitive gifted children may feel responsible for any disruption within the family, along with the financial burdens that ensue. Any pre-existing anxiety, perfectionism, or existential worries may increase. Some sensitive gifted children feel undeserving of the attention; others feel intense pressure to "pay back" their parents' expenditure through their efforts; no amount of ambivalence or slacking off is allowed.

> *Josh is often consumed with guilt and embarrassment when he thinks about his parents' sacrifices. When he was ten, they moved to a different city where he could receive a better education from a highly respected magnet school. His mother quit her job so that they could move, and never found one she liked after that. His father took a salary cut. His older sister blamed him for uprooting the family and was angry that she had to leave her friends. Josh pursued a degree in engineering during college, aware that his parents wanted him to be successful—even though he was much more interested in graphic design. He believed that he needed to "pay them back" for their sacrifices by landing a lucrative, stable, and well-respected job rather than following his own dreams.*

In the example above, Josh's parents did not pressure him or try to induce guilt. But as a perceptive and sensitive gifted child, he was aware of the stressors their sacrifice imposed on the family. His parents were in a bind—either they change the family situation or allow their son to languish in a school that could not meet his educational needs. They had pursued all possible advocacy channels, with little success. They made the best possible decision for their family at that time—even though it left Josh feeling confused and undeserving. Josh might have benefitted, though, from an open conversation about the emotional burden he was assuming. It can be hard for children to formulate what they are feeling, and even harder to express it. When parents anticipate and openly express what they suspect their child is feeling, the relief is palpable. For example, if Josh's parents had shared that they take full responsibility for the move and would never want him to feel guilty about it, he might have let go of his perceived burden. *"We know that we might seem frazzled as we settle into this new home. But we are so happy we moved, and we never would want you to feel any responsibility for our decision. Of course, we want the best for you and hope your new school will work out. But this was* our *decision, and we are excited to have this new opportunity for all of us."*

Of course, there are times when parents resort to harsh measures to propel their child ahead. When a child exhibits exceptional talent, parents may feel compelled to push them excessively, regardless of the potential emotional cost. Some parents lose all perspective and resort to extreme demands and belittle or bribe their child to succeed. Assor and Tal[17], for example, found that adolescents developed problematic coping styles if parents focused too much on achievement and only expressed positive reactions when their child succeeded. They claimed that this leads to "non-optimal self-esteem dynamics, in which people vacillate between feelings of grandiosity following success and self-derogation and shame following failure, which in turn promote a rigid and stressful mode of coping" (p. 249). An extreme example of parental expectations gone awry is portrayed in the relationship between famed pianist Lang Lang and his father. In an interview with The Guardian[18], Lang Lang described his memory of a low point in their relationship at age nine. His father was so frustrated with what seemed like a setback in Lang Lang's progress that he told him to kill himself! Clearly, this example is quite extreme and abusive. However, it can be tempting to demand excellence when your child seems bound for greatness. While many parents would cringe at the thought of assuming the role of a pushy parent, it may be hard to resist applying at least *some* pressure in an effort to support such potential.

Shepherding gifted children through the developmental, social, and emotional challenges of childhood—and supporting their outstanding abilities and talents—demands an enormous balancing act. Each decision may feel unnecessarily fraught with urgency. More than half (51.7%) of parents in the Gifted Parenting Survey reported feeling uncertain "a lot" or "always" about how much to push their child to excel. As one parent commented: *"[I am] worried that we are expecting too much. It's often hard to remember that he is just a child because he's so intelligent."* It may be difficult to gauge when expectations will create too much of an emotional toll. Recent articles[19,20] have lamented an increase in suicides at elite colleges and high schools, where any underlying depression and insecurity are amplified within a pressure-cooker culture. It is important to note that parental expectations, peer pressure, and academic demands do not *cause* depression or suicidal intent; multiple situational, genetic, and biochemical factors contribute to this level of distress. Nevertheless, some children succumb to external pressures and can feel overwhelmed. Remaining attuned to *how much* to push your child and what is excessive (based on your child's unique needs at the time) is essential. Your increased self-awareness related to goals, hopes, dreams, fears, and expectations for your child can provide direction and greater clarity.

What you should know about expectations

What is most important—as in all things parenting—is an understanding of your child's unique needs and a willingness to engage in direct, open communication. Consider your child's interests, temperament, emotional reactivity, motivational struggles, responsiveness to guidance, developmental level, and drive to achieve. Your self-awareness is equally important as you explore your wishes, fears, expectations, and the value you place on their potential success. We influence our children more than we might imagine. Sometimes, it is difficult to appreciate that our well-intentioned hopes, dreams, and wishes instill subtle influences that shape their behaviors. Even if you do not express it directly, a sensitive gifted child will sense your emotional investment in their achievements and may push themselves just to please you. So, how do you know if your encouragement is helpful, or merely a knee-jerk reaction based on your own needs? The following are some questions to consider. As mentioned above, please consider these questions with a spirit of curiosity and self-compassion. None of us are perfect. We all make mistakes and carry regrets. Consider these questions as a means of achieving greater self-understanding.

○ Do you set unrealistically high goals for your child? Are you expecting too much? Your child may have tremendous talent and potential, but their pace, drive, and interests may be quite different from what you expect. Do you compare your child's accomplishments to those of other gifted children and feel frustrated that your child is not as successful? Comparisons to other children can foster resentment and insecurity in your child and create frustration for you.

○ Do you sometimes use misguided motivational tactics? Do you regret resorting to harsh words or using shaming statements and criticism to try to motivate your child? While you may have learned that a firm approach is effective, it can generate immediate compliance but not the self-sufficiency and intrinsic drive that sparks persistence and true motivation. The best learning comes from excitement, inspiration, and intrinsic desire, not drudgery or a "boot camp" approach.

○ Are your child's accomplishments overly important to you? Have their achievements become the repository for your hopes and dreams, or a do-over for successes you wished you had achieved? Are you placing too much of your own self-worth on your child's successes? Would you feel devastated if your child did not live up to their potential?

○ Are you responding to pressure from your family of origin's expectations? Do you feel you have to meet someone else's approval by ensuring that your child succeeds? Are you worried others will view you as negligent for *not* pushing your child enough? On the other hand, are you holding back on encouraging your child to succeed because of worries about potential judgment from other parents?

If you recognize yourself in any of the above examples, it may be time to reevaluate your expectations. It is critical to understand, challenge, and resolve any of the underlying reasons that might drive over-involvement or place excessive pressure on your child—or, conversely, any reluctance to set goals and limits when appropriate. Our job as parents couples empathy and attunement with the sometimes unpleasant task of limit-setting. Children become angry; they rebel and resist. But as the "adults in the room," it falls on us to guide them. Many parents find themselves weighing the costs and benefits of their decisions on a daily basis. As you grapple with your degree of involvement in any given decision, you may want to consider the following questions:

1. **How important is the immediate task?** If the particular task is important, your involvement may be necessary. For example, submitting a college scholarship application by the deadline is more critical than completing a fifth-grade book report. Your child's age, temperament, and emotional adjustment need to be considered along with the significance of the immediate goals. There are times when they may need your strong encouragement, and others when it may be best to step back and allow them to take the lead… even if they fail.

2. **Does my involvement help or hinder their progress?** Sometimes kids get stuck. They feel lost, insecure, and anxious. They procrastinate, exaggerate the significance of any failures, or underestimate how much effort is necessary to succeed. Parents are there to guide them. You may need

to intervene and provide some support, limit-setting, or goal-setting. Daily variations in motivation, based on mood, distractions, waning interest, or even burn-out need to be considered. Sometimes, your child may respond positively to structure, strong encouragement, and limit-setting, and at other times, argue, rebel, and refuse to cooperate. You know your child best and can determine what type of involvement might work (such as gentle encouragement, humor, or setting firm limits). You *also* may sense when your involvement will backfire. A brief initial outburst where you child complains about your involvement can be expected. What is more problematic is if your child starts to rely on you completely, rebels and refuses to comply, shows signs of anxiety or depression, or gives up entirely.

3. **What is the long-term impact of my involvement?** As you sort through how much to intervene, keep in mind long-term goals. You might think that applying pressure and setting exceptionally high expectations "builds character" and instills habits that lead to further success. While some children may rise to the challenge, others may exhibit signs of insecurity, risk-avoidance, perfectionism, excessive reliance on you for guidance, or eventual rebellion. Many gifted children who are underachievers feel pressured to succeed and give up completely when faced with their perceived inadequacies.

Children recognize when encouragement to reach their potential makes sense, or when the goal is beyond their reach. Gifted children, with their perceptiveness and heightened sense of fairness and justice, become disillusioned if they believe they are merely accommodating the school's requirements or their parents' personal goals. If you hope to build independence, resilience, and confidence in your child, remaining attuned to their unique needs and determining how much to expect from them is essential. This includes paying attention to the present moment—to what your child needs now rather than exclusively focusing on future endeavors. Most gifted children want to excel; however, insecurity, perfectionism, and fears get in the way. Your sensitivity and attunement to their limitations and self-doubts conveys that you love and respect them, regardless of their accomplishments. Nevertheless, you can share your observation that they thrive when immersed in what interests them most, and that you are there to offer encouragement, provide accountability, if needed, and help them overcome any self-doubt that interferes with their progress. Clear, direct communication is essential; misunderstandings or feelings of resentment can be overcome when you both discuss the expectations in question and come to a reasonable compromise. Communication that combines love and empathy, a consideration of your child's input, and an understanding of their fears, will let them know that your expectations are in sync with their capabilities and intrinsic drive to succeed. In short, our task as parents involves recognizing, appreciating, and loving the child we have, along with managing our own expectations. As Silverman21 beautifully stated:

> "We have been called to help gifted children appreciate themselves, to follow their own paths, and to develop into emotionally healthy adults. Society needs their passion, their idealism, their creativity, their sensitivity, their problem-solving abilities. They are our future. We who cherish them have been entrusted with guiding and guarding the future of our planet. With our help, their gifts will become blessings to themselves and to the Universe" (p. 7).

What's next?

As noted in this chapter, high expectations can lead to comparisons with others. We all compare ourselves and our children to others at times. But sometimes, this can spark feelings of embarrassment or envy—difficult emotions to manage. The effects of comparisons on our child and on ourselves will be covered in the next chapter.

CHAPTER SIX

Comparing Your Child to Others

One thing parents of gifted children quickly realize is that their child is, well...*different*. Although bursting with intellectual smarts, astonishing talents, creativity, empathy, and insatiable curiosity, they also frequently manifest traits that can be a challenge. Many struggle with deficits in executive functioning skills that create roadblocks to success. Some underachieve, despite their capabilities. Still others struggle in their relationships with peers; impatient, socially awkward, immature, or discouraged by social norms that make no sense to them. While others may be in awe of your child's abilities, they also observe the quirks and delays. And as they witness behaviors consistent with asynchronous development, they scratch their heads. *How can such an advanced child seem so immature? How can such a smart kid lack common sense?* You may have trouble finding adults who "get it" and with whom you can commiserate or share your fears and worries.

Parents of gifted children may experience feelings of joy and pride, but they also endure troubling emotions at times—embarrassment and envy that arise when comparing their child to others. All parents make comparisons; it goes with the territory. You watch your friend's child taking their first step while yours is still crawling. You are amazed when your cousin's three-year-old displays manners your much older child would never grasp. Although you recognize that all children differ, with varying strengths and challenges, it is tough to watch your child struggle or lag behind their peers. It can be painful to navigate these troubling emotions. You want to appreciate and accept your child completely, quirks and all, yet you cannot help but compare. The dichotomy between their remarkable talents and their social immaturity or asynchronous development can be daunting. And when your child accomplishes something astounding, but other kids take center stage, it leaves you wilted, confused, and perhaps, feeling guilty about your reactions. As a result, parents of gifted children struggle with powerful emotions—with few outlets for support.

Embarrassment

It takes courage to admit that we sometimes feel embarrassed about our child. Of course, all parents can feel embarrassment; when their child creates a disruption in the classroom, for example, or cries through their friend's birthday party. Parents of gifted children experience the same emotions as other parents whose children disappoint. The difference lies in expectations associated with your gifted child's abilities. While they may exhibit amazing talents that fill you with pride, at other times, you cringe. You may want to hide when your child melts down in public, behaves immaturely, cannot get along with children their age, or is disrespectful to others. When their intellect is so high, it is particularly hard to witness signs of asynchronous development, immaturity, acting out, tantrums, or rude behavior toward other adults or children. It is not only frustrating, but hard to explain to those who do not understand, especially when your child says something brilliant one minute, and then acts regressively the next. The following examples are typical:

> *My five-year-old still has meltdowns in public when he is tired. It is embarrassing when we're at the check-out line at a store and he can add up the items in the cart, but is whining and carrying on like a two-year-old while he waits.*

> *My daughter is oblivious about what she wears, and doesn't care if she fits in. She raises her hand in class all the time, corrects the other kids, and generally annoys them. I wish she would try harder to get along with them.*

My child constantly challenges his teacher. Most of the time, it is because he refuses to censor his thoughts and opinions. For example, he points out when the teacher's instruction differs from what was in the textbook. Unfortunately, his teacher is not thrilled with his insights and views him as disrespectful. While my son may be "correct" in his comments, he seems unable to overlook her shortcomings, and ends up alienating himself from her.

You might hate to admit it, but sometimes you might wish that your child was just "normal." You worry about their social and emotional development and whether they will find friends who are truly accepting. *Will she get bullied because she is different? Will it upset him if he only has a few friends? Will she miss out on high school social events like dances and parties?* You adore your child and are in awe of their abilities, but you often wish they were like other children their age… if they could just get along with kids in the neighborhood…if they were less sensitive and emotionally intense…if you didn't have to explain and sometimes apologize for their offbeat behavior. It seems that life would be easier for your child—*and* for you—if so much additional energy was not required. Parents frequently feel alone with their reactions, as other parents often cannot understand or relate to the challenges they face.

Kara was at the playground with her nine-year-old child, James. There was a sand volleyball court and James was playing with the other kids. Then she looked over and noticed (with horror and embarrassment) that her son was now sitting down on the court, practically at the net, and playing in the sand. The other kids were trying to ignore him at first and play around him. James always was fascinated with sandcastles. But his obliviousness to disrupting the game was mortifying. She quickly called him over so he could leave the game and avoid the wrath of the other kids just trying to play volleyball. Her friend tried to help her to shrug it off, but Kara still felt embarrassed.

As mentioned in Chapter 2, asynchronous development is a hallmark feature of giftedness and infuses social interactions with an unsettling level of uncertainty. Intellectually advanced children often behave as if they were many years younger than their given age. Many of the most embarrassing situations parents experience often stem from this discrepancy between intellect and maturity. Silverman[1] has described the difficulties faced by the highly gifted, who struggle to fit into social norms not designed for them, and suggested that "asynchrony is both a blessing and a curse" (p. 6).

Embarrassment often is rooted in feelings of shame. We feel shame when we attribute an action or behavior to what we fear is a deeply flawed part of ourselves. Guilt differs from shame in that it typically arises after we behave in a manner that conflicts with our values and contrasts with how we typically view ourselves. For example, you might feel a bit guilty after arguing with a salesclerk or if you lie to avoid a dreaded family gathering. We may not like feeling guilty but view the behavior as atypical and not grounded in our identity. Shame, on the other hand, reflects deeper feelings about our sense of self. It is more personal than guilt; it encompasses a broader, deeply negative view of who we are. According to Brene Brown[2], shame is "the intensely painful feeling or experience of believing that we are flawed and therefore unworthy of love and belonging." When we feel embarrassment about our gifted child's misbehavior, we might assume we are inadequate as parents since we could not prevent the offending behavior. We feel responsible for their actions. We also might worry about what others think, and fear that they also view us as "bad parents."

Most research on embarrassment among parents has studied families where the child exhibits problem behaviors associated with a specific diagnostic category. Some examples include embarrassment reported by parents whose children are autistic[3,4], who experience mental health disorders[5,6], who struggle with drug abuse[7], or engage in self-harming behaviors[8]. In these situations, parents often feel isolated, fear that society will blame them, or worry that they are entirely responsible for their child's behaviors. Unfortunately, feelings of embarrassment and shame perpetuate further isolation, as parents try to keep their emotions to themselves rather than search for the support they need.

It can be difficult to acknowledge your embarrassment. *After all, how can I feel embarrassed by my own child, who is not always responsible for these behaviors?* Yet, feelings of embarrassment are understandable and common. In fact, *all* parents experience some feelings of frustration or grief over not having the "perfect" child they had envisioned. And it is understandable to wish that life could be easier for you and your child, or that your child would not have to suffer because of differences or misunderstandings. Embarrassment only becomes problematic if it persists and interferes with a loving attachment to your child, causes feelings of depression, or contributes to pressuring your child unnecessarily, especially if your "perfect child" fantasies involve highly unattainable goals. As noted previously, the more we are aware of our expectations and reactions, the easier we can manage them. Here are a few questions for self-reflection:

- ○ Why does my child use poor judgment or engage in embarrassing behaviors? For example, is it due to social immaturity, shyness, asynchronous development, difficulty accessing empathy for others who are different, or impulsivity? Can I view the embarrassing behavior as a signal that my child needs greater learning and support? For example, do they need help with social skills, perspective-taking (considering another person's viewpoint and motivations), containing their impulsivity, or calming feelings of anxiety? Do I need to approach these behaviors differently?

- ○ What situations evoke the greatest feelings of embarrassment? Is it when my child misbehaves in public, shows poor judgment, expresses uncensored opinions to an authority figure (such as their teacher), or seems to struggle socially? Does it occur only in the presence of certain people whom I worry might judge us?

- ○ How much of my embarrassment is tied to assumptions related to my child's giftedness and my frustration because of such a discrepancy between intellectual abilities and maturity or social skills?

○ What am I most afraid others will think? Am I concerned that they will dislike or misunderstand my child or judge me negatively as a parent?

○ How have I coped with feelings of embarrassment in the past? Does it haunt me and create anxiety or dread, or am I able to put it behind me? Do I tend to feel shame or assume others are exceptionally focused on my mistakes?

○ What would need to change so that I could laugh off embarrassing situations? What would it take to feel confident enough to share my worries and concerns with trusted friends? What would allow me to feel confident challenging others who may be judging or misinterpreting my child's behaviors?

After considering the questions above, it may be helpful to develop a plan for coping with feelings of embarrassment. As noted previously, we all feel embarrassed at times. Often, we can laugh at our goofy mistakes. The ability to place our missteps in perspective can be difficult, though. Rather than defensiveness or denial, we need to enlist self-compassion and an acceptance that everyone struggles and makes mistakes. Learning to forgive ourselves for our fallibility and imperfections is the first step. After that, developing the capacity to put embarrassing situations in perspective is essential. We often place too much emphasis on our imperfections and assume that others are judging us. As with anything distressing, finding support from trusted friends and family can provide relief. While you might be worrying and overthinking about an embarrassing situation, those who know you best can place it in context and help you move past your worries.

Embarrassment over your child's behavior is one step removed from your sense of yourself as a parent. When your child embarrasses you, it can be hard to believe that your parenting abilities are not under review. We often feel personally responsible when our child misbehaves or is disrespectful to others or cannot handle themselves in social situations. Even when our embarrassment is associated with our gifted child's lagging social maturity, we need to appreciate that they are on their own path. We can guide them with respect to appropriate social behavior, empathy, respect for others, and attention to social cues. However, if our child struggles socially, we need to accept this reality. Appreciation and gratitude for our child's amazing qualities (irrespective of giftedness) can place problem behaviors in perspective. Enlisting feelings of acceptance for our child—imperfections and all—will remind us of what we appreciate most.

Envy

When you love your child, you want the best for them. And comparing their achievements and social acumen to other children's accomplishments is a natural consequence of your love. After all, how can you *not* compare? You are your child's champion, cheerleader, and biggest fan. Yet even though they might breeze through classes and excel at various skills, you still may feel pangs of envy toward other families and their children. It is difficult to sit by and idly watch as your child's classmates surpass them, even when their accomplishments also deserve recognition. You may strive for compassion and humility, but at times, competitive feelings, bitterness, and even rage can take hold.

When your child accomplishes something astounding but other children take center stage, it can evoke feelings of envy. When other families seem to have every advantage, you might stew inside. However, these initial reactions leave you feeling uneasy and a bit guilty. *Why should I feel resentful because some other child gets an award? Why can't I accept that other families can afford to send their children to private school, even if we cannot? When will I stop comparing my child to the other kids who seem to have so many friends?* These thoughts and feelings aren't pretty, but they are normal and understandable.

Our feelings of guilt are a reminder that something is amiss; we need to recognize how envy fuels bitterness and is incongruous with our values. What counts is how we handle these reactions. Do they persist and torment us, or can we learn from them and achieve some semblance of acceptance? Envy and bitterness can arise when opportunities seem out of reach, when someone seems to have all the luck in the world, or when their success seems undeserved. Some comparisons that incite envy include the following: comparing your child to other children who seem socially poised and popular, who win awards, who are well-liked by their teachers, or who never seem to struggle with depression or anxiety; comparing yourself to other parents who can afford private schools or intensive enrichment experiences, who have the time and inclination to homeschool, or who are more vocal at school, seemingly unencumbered by insecurity or hesitation; comparing yourself to anyone who has more wealth, success, beauty, talent, or a seemingly "perfect" marriage. The list could go on.

Envy arises even more intensively during times of heightened competition. Any event involving awards, recognition or competition will invite comparisons. *How did she get that award? I don't think she really deserved it. I bet her parents helped her with that project.* Competition often reaches a frenzied pace when the stakes are high—particularly with college admissions or scholarship opportunities. While you might aspire to an attitude of calm acceptance, if you suspect that another child had an unfair advantage, or that your child was slighted by a college admissions department, strong feelings can arise. *He probably got in because his parents donated money to the college. I bet her parents spent a fortune on SAT prep classes.* Your envy also may unintentionally influence your child's opinions. They might sense your reaction and either join in (*Yeah, you're right, she doesn't deserve that award!*), or may blame themselves (*I guess I can't compare to those other kids—I'm just not good enough.*). While your reactions may be prompted out of love for your child, blaming other children for their successes or good fortune is troubling. For example, if a teacher favors another child, and you feel that your child was unfairly treated, the blame lies with the teacher—not the other student. As much as we might dislike one of our child's classmates, or resent their apparent success, we must take a deep breath and remind ourselves that they are *children*—all struggling, striving, and navigating their way through childhood.

Feelings of envy may be unrelated to your child's giftedness, though. You might envy another child's athletic abilities, physical attractiveness, warmth, social confidence, or respectful behavior toward their parents. You might wish that your child did not struggle with heightened sensitivities, or perfectionism, or obsessive thinking. You view other children who seem more "normal" and wonder what life must be like in a more relaxed household. And then, you kick yourself for having these thoughts.

> *Jessica swallowed her resentment as her friend's daughter continued to receive invitations to every classmate's birthday party, while her own daughter only was invited to two of them. Yes, the other little girl is outgoing and fun to be with. Jessica's daughter is shy, serious, and often more interested in science projects than playing with her classmates. Jessica hated the fact that she envied her friend; however, she could not quell her rising feelings of resentment.*

Envy is a natural, but uncomfortable and sometimes destructive emotion. It fuels anger and bitterness, may incite hateful thoughts toward unsuspecting children and families, and leaves us feeling depleted and full of shame. It arises when we feel insecure, emotionally unfulfilled, or deprived. Idealization of something outside of ourselves is required; we compare ourselves to others, cannot appreciate what is already wonderful about ourselves, and end up feeling less worthwhile in comparison. It also can be a defense against shame, as we might worry that our suspected inadequacies will be discovered. Rather than appreciating and feeling good about ourselves—or our children—we focus on how we never have enough and must attain something more. *If I achieve what* they *have, I will feel better about myself.* Unsurprisingly, envy is associated with an increased risk for depression[9]. Burton[10] outlined the conditions that are necessary for envy to arise:

> "To feel envy, three conditions need to be met. First, we must be confronted with a person (or persons) with something—a possession, quality, or achievement—that has eluded us. Second, we must desire that something for ourselves. And third, we must be personally pained by the associated emotion."

In a longitudinal study of the impact of envy, Mujcic and Oswald[11] reported an association between envy and worsening mental health or well-being over time. A review of the literature[12] also indicated that social comparisons were associated with anxiety and depression. When we cannot accept our circumstances or feel gratitude for what we have, it is easy to compare and assume others have it better. Often, we ignore or discount the possible hardships those we envy might endure. Perhaps that neighbor with the beautiful home suffers through long hours at work just to pay the mortgage. Perhaps children who seem so well-behaved in public struggle with anxiety and are terrified of repercussions if they misbehave. Perhaps students who attend prestigious private schools are sometimes less content than your own public school educated child. That phrase, "the grass is always greener" comes to mind.

Some people become accustomed to feeling envy toward others who seem more fortunate. Anyone who has endured an abusive childhood, poverty, racism, inequity, serious health conditions, early childhood losses, or lack of opportunities may become envious and even bitter in the face of so much bounty. When you have struggled and endured hardship, it is understandable to long for what seems like an easy life filled with wealth and opportunities. Whether those fantasies are valid or not, comparing yourself to others will make you feel worse. You might feel justified in your resentment; ultimately, though, envy fuels divisiveness, bitterness, and additional feelings of despair. The many books, films, and TV series depicting wealthy but highly dysfunctional families are, no doubt, grounded in a widespread desire to see those more fortunate struggle just as much as the rest of us. Regardless of our financial or social status, though, anyone can experience feelings of envy, especially if they feel emotionally wounded or deprived.

A close cousin to envy is bitterness. Envy and bitterness are a natural consequence when another's success seems unjust or inequitable. Gifted children and adults often abhor social injustice and possess a strong sense of fairness. When you suspect that someone obtained their good fortune through nefarious means, by "stepping on" the little guy, or through manipulation, it is understandable that you might feel bitter about their success. Bitterness also may arise when an individual's acclaim, success, or popularity emanates from a seemingly arbitrary advantage. For example, it might seem unfair that your child's classmate gained admission to an elite college, presumably due to legacy status, or that a neighbor's artwork hangs in a prestigious gallery, possibly facilitated through family connections with the gallery owner. These situations are complicated, as they invoke less envy toward the individual, but instead target those in power who set the rules, or who supply the coveted opportunities. On a smaller scale, when another student in your gifted child's class receives accolades for their accomplishments—and your child is overlooked—it makes sense that you might feel bitter, although your bitterness may be directed toward the school's policy regarding awards or recognition rather than the other child.

> *John was furious that his son was ignored for the varsity wrestling team's MVP award and scholarship. His son was clearly an outstanding athlete and showed leadership and compassion toward his teammates. However, he missed two games because of school commitments with the debate team. The rules were clear; the award only was offered if there was perfect attendance. John was aware of this rule but felt bitter since the rule seemed rigid and unfairly penalized his son because of academic commitments. He did not begrudge his son's teammate who won the award, but felt sad, angry, and deflated that his son's accomplishments were not recognized.*

Not all forms of envy are bad, though. Researchers Van der Ven and colleagues[13] have differentiated malicious envy (which fuels bitterness, anger, and a desire for sabotage or a wish to harm others) from benign envy (where envy is used as a motivational tool and is not associated with harm toward another). In reality, there are some people who are much more accomplished and successful. When we believe that their success is deserved, we may be inspired by their accomplishments and strive toward achieving the same goals. In essence, we can grow through comparisons with others if we manage the intensity of our feelings. Psychoanalytic theorists also have conceptualized how feelings of envy can be transformed into positive motivation. Zell[14] has theorized that envy can be "reshaped into constructive achievement strivings," and Ninivaggi[15] stated the following: "Envy, recognized and intelligently managed, transforms and may spur admiration, emulation, aspiration, empathy, and developmental advantages." Lange and Crusius[16] studied envy among marathon runners. The researchers found that when compared with runners who felt malicious envy toward an elite runner, those who instead felt benign envy and admiration improved their race performance by using the elite runners as role models and then modifying their own goals. When envy is placed in perspective, and is devoid of bitterness and anger, it can serve as motivation to work harder and accomplish what is attainable.

I would propose that there is a third component to envy—a healthy acceptance that we cannot have everything we want, that life has its ups and downs, and that sometimes, other people seem to have it better. We all suffer disappointments, grief, and loss. Even the motivational approaches mentioned above may not necessarily apply. Depending on the circumstances, we cannot always strive for something different; sometimes, we must come to terms with our unique situation and accept what we have. Finding contentment and acceptance, along with gratitude for our own (and our child's) good fortune is an antidote to envy.

> *Julie struggled with the empty nest, especially after her youngest completed college. With her blessings, her children all followed their chosen career paths, where they landed in distant cities. She was proud of them and never would interfere or pressure them to move back to their hometown. Yet, she envied other families whose children lived nearby. She had to accept that her children's trajectory was different from others and learn to cope with her sadness and grief rather than brooding over comparisons. She also reminded herself that some of her friends' adult children were not as fortunate as her own, as many of them still relied on their parents for financial support or were struggling in their careers. Instead of feeling envious, she tried to focus more on gratitude for what her family has.*

What can you do when feelings of envy arise?

1. **First, take a deep breath and recognize that envy is normal and understandable.** Appreciate that it stems from your love and passion for your child. If you didn't care so much, you would not feel so envious. So, give yourself a break.

2. **Second, challenge your thoughts about how the situation will affect your child.** Is it essential that they win or succeed most of the time? Can they accept a loss—even when those in authority seem unfair? Is there something they can learn from the experience? Can they develop resilience and feel compassion for others who also may be just as deserving of success? Can your child use these experiences to solidify their resolve to work harder next time?

3. **Evaluate your own need to win.** Why is it so important that your child receive recognition? Yes, of course it may seem unfair if they are overlooked, but other children deserve acknowledgement also. Can you learn to tolerate disappointment? Can you put any loss in perspective so that you can move on and help your child accept the loss?

4. **On the other hand, consider taking constructive action to remedy a problematic situation.** When envy or bitterness stem from an injustice or a wrong that must be addressed, you can enlist your underlying anger as a springboard for pursuing change. For example, if your child's academic needs are repeatedly ignored at school, rather than envying those students who seem more "appealing" to the teacher, use your energy toward addressing the teacher's attitude. We may resent that our child does not receive the educational services they need; transforming our anger and bitterness into an advocacy plan, though, allows us to initiate change and reduces feelings of hopelessness. We also serve as a role model for our children; they learn that tactful and strategic action are an antidote to envy and bitterness. Like the marathoners in the study listed above, children can learn that they

can transform envy and bitterness into positive action that can result in either personal or systemic change.

5. **Learn to accept your child's imperfections.** You need to accept who your child is—not pine for the fantasy child you desired. This may involve grieving over the fact that you may never have the dream child you wanted. We all have heard of "soccer parents," for example, screaming from the sidelines and urging their child to excel, even if the child is disinterested or not particularly athletic. Most of us assume we are more attuned to our child's needs and would not push them to accomplish something unattainable. Nevertheless, it still stings when we wish for qualities in our child that they do not possess. Like all children, yours will disappoint you at some point. Developing tolerance for your child's differences, limitations, struggles, quirks, and sometimes puzzling decisions can feel like an endurance challenge. But the sooner you accept this, the better you will feel.

6. **Consider practicing mindfulness.** Researchers Dong and colleagues[17], for example, found that malicious envy (the form of envy where frustration fuels a desire for sabotage or harm toward others) was negatively associated with both psychological resilience and mindfulness. A mindfulness practice can keep you focused on what is present right now— for you, for your child, and for whatever is happening in your current life situation. A mindfulness practice suppresses some of the strivings and longing for more that ultimately leaves us feeling unfulfilled. Many apps, videos, and classes on mindfulness are available, and some schools are now even teaching mindfulness to their students.

7. **Consider your perspective, thoughts, and feelings related to envy—and then take action.** Do you really want to feel miserable, waste your time, or denigrate yourself because of bitterness over someone else's accomplishments or good fortune? When you notice feelings of envy, can you change

gears and actively consider putting your reactions into perspective? When you envy someone's inherited wealth, for example, can you remind yourself of the many people who would wish for *your* lifestyle, especially those who are less fortunate? When you resent that your child was overlooked for an award at school, instead of resenting the child who won, can you consider addressing inequities in the school system that led to their choices? Can you help your child place a loss or seemingly unfair decision into perspective, and use it as a learning experience? Keep in mind that holding onto envy only leaves you feeling miserable; it does not change the situation. Do you *really* want to feel miserable? Life is not fair at times; losing is painful, but an experience with loss can enhance resilience for coping with later setbacks. And your child has your wisdom available to guide them through their disappointment.

8. **The most difficult challenge of all may involve cultivating compassion toward those you envy.** Keep in mind that accomplishments and success often carry a heavy burden. While your child may be shut out of an opportunity, the child who "won" may have struggled and suffered along the way. Wealthy families experience the same sadness and losses as everyone else. Olympic athletes who achieve fame and financial success sometimes endure crushing depression when their minute in the spotlight recedes. The parable of the Buddha and the mustard seed is a useful reminder. A woman who was distraught with grief came to the Buddha asking for special consideration. She was instructed to first obtain a mustard seed from a family that had not experienced grief and loss. She knocked on every door and eventually realized that *every* family had suffered.

In summary...

One of our greatest challenges as parents involves recognizing when we compare our child to others, and then, learning to cope with the uncomfortable feelings that arise. Yes, sometimes comparisons contribute to feelings of pride, as we are reminded of our child's gifts and talents. But wise parents realize these emotions are fleeting, as there always will be someone who will surpass your child. We must recognize when comparisons generate a level of embarrassment that alienates us from our child and evokes resentment and shame. We also must appreciate that while envy is a normal reaction, it can make us miserable, and we may transmit these negative emotions and opinions to our child. Acknowledging another family's or child's "right" to succeed is essential. Learning to accept that the school, community, and even your family members may let you down is an important life lesson. When we weather and rebound from disappointments, we also role model healthy resilience for our child. Most importantly, cultivating gratitude and an appreciation for *your* child—shortcomings and all—is essential.

What's next?

While embarrassment and envy are tough emotions to handle, other feelings may be even more troubling. All parents experience anxiety, fear, disappointment, and regret. And although these are universal emotions, parents of gifted children may have difficulty placing their emotional reactions in context. The next chapter explores these normal and understandable, although distressing feelings, and how parents can adapt and channel their emotions so that they are less troubled by them.

CHAPTER SEVEN
Troubling Emotions

One of the unspoken truths about gifted parenting is the ubiquity of troubling emotions. Anxiety, disappointment, frustration, regret, guilt—these emotions are all too familiar to most parents of gifted children. Although clearly distressing, they are normal, understandable, *and predictable*. Most parents of the gifted are on this journey without a roadmap—struggling to keep up with their child's intellectual needs, quirks, intensity, and social challenges. As noted previously, parents often feel isolated and even abandoned, as well-intentioned teachers, friends, and extended family offer little guidance. Parenting is hard enough; feeling different from other families, realizing that traditional parenting advice does not always work for your child, and having few outlets for support take their toll. As a result, parents of gifted children often struggle in silence as they grapple with their own fears and distress.

We all possess learned, engrained coping styles when faced with difficult, emotionally challenging situations[1]. Coping styles can be healthy or unhealthy depending on the situation and the ultimate outcome. Distraction, for example, can be a healthy coping strategy for interrupting obsessive worrying, but a problem when it interferes with our responsibilities (like paying the bills on time!). Segerstrom and Smith[2] have proposed four coping styles that commonly occur when faced with difficult emotions: approach, escape, avoidance, or attempt to control. We all have preferred, go-to coping strategies, although we may use different, less familiar approaches under duress. Someone who typically withdraws and avoids conflict may erupt in anger toward an offender when pushed too far. Someone who overthinks and tries to gain control over stressful situations may retreat into feelings of despair and hopelessness when they encounter too many roadblocks. It is not surprising that our preferred coping styles affect how we approach parenting and any distressing emotions that arise. Consider how your coping strategies relate to some of the commonly experienced troubling emotions described in the following sections.

Anxiety

Parenting is hard enough; raising a gifted child gives rise to unexpected challenges. In fact, most new parents feel some anxiety about the daunting task of child-raising. However, parents of gifted children face additional demands, and many experience fears, worries, and outright panic when they think of the road ahead. *Am I doing this right? Will I help my child find the academic opportunities she needs? How do I know whether to push him or let him progress at his own pace? Should I enroll her in enrichment activities or just let her relax after school? And why isn't there any clearcut advice about this?*

Early awareness of your toddler's or preschooler's abilities may spark apprehension about their future. Concerns may increase once your child enters school and languishes in classes that seem devoid of challenge or stimulation. You may worry that your child will become disengaged, lose respect for the school, underachieve, or at the very least, fail to develop essential executive functioning skills. You might brood over how you can best advocate for your child, how to approach the teacher, and whether your advocacy efforts will make any difference at all. You might even question whether you have the competence, knowledge, assertiveness, or stamina to advocate effectively. And your concerns can morph into fears that your gifted child will never reach their potential.

> *Michael hated conflict, having been raised in a highly argumentative family. Although advocacy was necessary to ensure that his daughter would receive gifted services, he avoided anything other than polite conversation with her teacher at conferences. He worried that asserting his concerns would cause too many problems, so he held back. Unfortunately,*

his daughter never received the services she needed, started to hate school, and refused to complete assignments she viewed as meaningless.

Concerns about academics do not stop after grade school, of course. You might question how much to push your adolescent child and when to retreat, especially since grades matter more in high school. You might worry about your child's high school course selection, whether it is challenging enough (or conversely, if it is too stressful), and how it will affect college admissions. Parents question whether to advocate for their child or encourage their child's independence and expect them to advocate for themselves. Yet even with older children or teens, parents sometimes must remain involved. For example, you may be more qualified to guide your child in their college search than the school's guidance counselor (who may have little experience with gifted teens). And the college applications and admissions process ushers in its own set of worries, along with anxiety about financial burdens and the empty nest ahead.

Your anxiety might extend to your child's social well-being, especially if they exhibit signs of asynchronous development, social immaturity, or reside in a community where there are few like-minded peers. It breaks your heart as you watch your child lurking on the outskirts of the playground, unable to engage with the other kids. Aware that early social differences may transition into shyness and isolation from peers at a later age, you might project your fears well into the future and envision a variety of disturbing scenarios. *Will she get bullied because she is different? What if he only finds a few friends? Will she miss out on high school social events, like dances and parties? How will he navigate friendships in college when he can't seem to find friends now?*

What likely fuels the greatest anxiety, though, is your gifted child's emotional well-being. While social challenges may create distress, some of their suffering also stems from their internal world. Many of the meltdowns and behavioral problems seen during the early years can be tied to heightened overexcitabilities or asynchronous development. The emotional storms of early childhood are powerful and upsetting to witness. As gifted children mature, their ability to ponder the meaning of life, their outrage over social injustice, and their outlier status among peers may contribute to deeper levels of distress. Some may have high hopes for eradicating wrongs and social injustice but feel powerless and give up trying. It can be devastating to watch your child's distress and possible struggles with depression, anxiety, low self-esteem, perfectionism, existential angst, social insecurity, apathy, or the repercussions of heightened emotional reactivity and sensitivity. Even worse, you may feel helpless when their emotional distress is exacerbated by peer influences or unavoidable academic pressures.

There are few studies that investigate stress among parents of gifted children; however, what research exists points to increased levels of stress and anxiety. Both McDowell[3] and Free[4] have highlighted the stress and anxiety parents face when teachers and other professionals ignore their child's academic needs. In a study comparing parents of gifted children to those with neurotypical children, Rimmlinger[5] found higher levels of anxiety among parents of the gifted. Stress levels were most elevated if the child exhibited oppositional behaviors or if parents were unable to find a school that met their child's academic needs. Rimmlinger proposed that their stress was comparable to what is seen among parents of children with a developmental delay and emphasized that many gifted children should be viewed as having exceptionalities. This label would lend credibility to the very real struggles both gifted children and their parents face.

Anxiety and fear are powerful emotions, and when they arise, it may be difficult to separate our own worries from what might be best for our child. Anxiety can emerge in a variety of forms—an overall sense of foreboding, obsessive fears, repeated checking (*why aren't those grades listed yet?*), irritability, physical symptoms such as headaches or gastrointestinal distress, or even full-blown panic attacks. As human beings, we are equipped to quickly recognize a threatening situation. Essential for our species' survival, the most observant, attuned, and vigilant members within a community were the most likely to survive. They gathered information and watched for predators or threats of attack from invaders. Our sympathetic nervous system jumps into gear to protect us and readily accesses the fight, flight, or freeze response. Nevertheless, our modern-day worries are no match for battling sabertoothed tigers, and we rarely face serious threats to life and limb. Anxiety arises in the face of far less threatening situations, such as worrying about what to wear to an interview, forming dire predictions about failing an exam, and next-day rumination over our interactions at a friend's party. Our ancient warning system goes awry when it creates unnecessary distress, when it is ever-present, and when it is tethered to thoughts and situations that do not endanger us. Anxiety has a strong neurobiological component[6]. Some of us may be more prone to anxiety than others, whether due to a genetic or biochemical predisposition, family of origin influences, past trauma, or even a history of intergenerational trauma[7]. And, of course, anyone who resides in an abusive household or a neighborhood where threats of violence are commonplace must maintain a heightened level of vigilance. Ongoing sympathetic nervous system arousal can extract a heavy toll on one's psyche and physical health[8,9]. As mentioned earlier, gifted people (both children *and* their parents) tend to be a highly sensitive, emotionally reactive, and overthinking bunch—possessing all the ingredients for the emergence of anxiety.

Anxiety is uncomfortable, and when we are in distress, it makes sense to reach for a solution that might alleviate our discomfort. Sometimes our coping strategies ultimately contribute to even worse consequences, though. For example, a complete avoidance of much-feared social situations, frequent requests for reassurance, or reliance on alcohol or drugs are strategies that backfire. Problematic coping strategies also can affect our parenting efforts. When parenting decisions are heavily influenced by our own fears—and an overriding drive to minimize and calm these fears—our child's best interests may be ignored. While intending to protect or guide them, our efforts may cause more damage than good. If we worry excessively about our child's potential success, for example, we might pressure and coerce them to achieve in a manner that amplifies their stress. Conversely, we might resist taking action to address their limited enrichment opportunities at school if we are afraid of potential conflict. Sometimes, when fears loom large, we might limit our child's participation in age-appropriate activities, such as sleepovers, camp, or dating. Everyone struggles with anxiety, worries, and insecurity at times, and often there are no clear (or ideal) parenting options. Some worries and concerns may be warranted, depending on your child's peer group, social skills, emotional stability, and the safety of your neighborhood. Nevertheless, if we remain unaware of our go-to coping styles or if we frequently rely on unhealthy anxiety-reducing behaviors, we may miss opportunities to support our child's growth and development.

> *Susan felt overwhelmed with the responsibility of ensuring that her gifted daughter, Jenny, receive the education she needed. She enrolled her in enrichment activities every summer, even though Jenny begged her parents to let her go to sports camp. Susan was afraid that if her daughter did not get an edge up on learning, she would fall behind at school. Due to her anxiety, she did not listen to her daughter's desire to take a break from academics and spend summers focusing on sports. Jenny became resentful and argumentative, was furious that her parents seemed to discount her input, and started to lose interest in classes she had previously enjoyed.*

It is normal to worry when you love your child. It becomes a problem, though, when anxiety becomes excessive, interferes with your ability to function, or negatively affects your parenting decisions. Our job as parents requires learning how to contain and redirect our anxiety so that it does not interfere with parenting choices. The following questions should be considered with a spirit of self-discovery; please appreciate that these are common reactions, and not intended to criticize or contribute to self-blame.

○ Do you frequently envision dire circumstances that could befall your child? Does the anxiety pervade your daily life in a manner that feels intrusive? Do you feel nervous, on edge, or irritable? Do you have difficulty concentrating? Do you wish that you could stop obsessing and worrying so much? Is anxiety affecting you physically, manifesting in physical symptoms (headaches, digestive complaints), a loss of appetite, or difficulty sleeping?

○ Do you rely on mood-altering substances or unhealthy distractions to cope with your anxiety? Are you overeating, smoking, drinking too much alcohol, abusing prescription medications, using street drugs, overspending, or engaging in other unhealthy escape strategies to handle your feelings?

○ Does your anxiety contribute to an overreaction to your child's behaviors? Do you pressure your child to overprepare for exams, question them excessively about time spent with friends, or share your personal worries with them? Do you make decisions for them to ensure that *you* will not feel anxious, rather than considering what would be best for their growth and development?

○ Do your fears limit you from taking action when it is required? Are you reluctant to advocate, speak up, or challenge your child, spouse, family member or teacher when needed? Are you worried about what others may think, whether you are entitled to voice complaints, or if your comments will cause conflict?

○ Have trusted friends, family, or professionals (such as your physician, your child's pediatrician, a therapist) expressed concern about your anxiety or how your fears might affect your child? Are your reactions much more extreme than those of friends and family whom you respect and trust?

If you identified with some of the above questions, you are not alone. Most people can admit to experiencing many of these emotions or behaviors at some point in time. It becomes problematic, though, when anxiety persists or becomes a knee-jerk response that you cannot ignore. While some parents try to suppress and quietly weather their anxiety, many do not realize that children—especially bright, perceptive children—sense their parents' emotions. Children realize when parents hesitate, worry, feel afraid, or hold back. Anxiety may seem almost contagious at times; you might discover that your child now worries about the same potential threats you most fear.

Sara felt very anxious before her son's theatre performances. She tried to hide her feelings from him, but he still sensed her anxiety. Although he loved acting, he started to doubt his abilities, and what was once comfortable and natural for him, became stressful and tedious. He eventually gave up acting because it became much too stressful for him.

Many parents of gifted children also possess the same heightened sensitivities and physiological reactivity as their child. They have suffered the misery of anxiety and want to limit their child's exposure to stress. Yet, anxiety is tough to contain; unless we are highly attuned to our behaviors, and actively work on managing our fears, they may spill out in an unintended manner. Some parents—particularly those who have endured trauma or loss—may feel controlled by their fears. These are the parents who are highly overprotective and restrict their child from engaging in normative age-appropriate activities. In their efforts to protect their child, they overlook the social and emotional consequences of their decisions. They mean well but cannot see past their fears.

Marjorie endured a difficult childhood filled with verbal and physical abuse. She became fearful of situations she could not control. When her daughter, Carla, started to assert her independence, Marjorie insisted that Carla refrain from many social activities with her friends. Carla was interpersonally gifted and was highly attuned to others' feelings, social interactions, and what seemed a reasonable level of risk. She could not abide by her mother's prohibitions and fears about what seemed like normal behavior. Carla fought with her mother throughout middle school and high school. She became secretive and eventually rebelled by engaging in high-risk social behaviors. Marjorie's attempts to protect her daughter backfired because she was unable to manage her own fears.

In the example above, Marjorie never envisioned that her overprotective parenting might contribute to what she feared most. She loved her daughter and wanted to keep her safe. Yet, her overwhelming fears blinded her ability to clearly assess both her daughter's temperament and the social climate. She was unable to let go and allow her daughter to engage in socially normative behaviors, despite some inherent risks. Ideally, Marjorie would have sought guidance from trusted friends or a mental health professional. Anxiety is difficult enough; trying to cope with powerful emotions on our own is an impossible task.

Managing anxiety requires a toolbox full of approaches. Some may be preventative; others require both temporary and permanent lifestyle changes. There are thousands of articles and books available related to anxiety. Rather than recommend a particular book, I would suggest that you research what is available online or through your local bookstore or library. A variety of organizations also provide helpful guidance and support for managing anxiety, such as the National Alliance on Mental Illness, the American Psychological Association, the American Counseling Association, the Anxiety and Depression Association of America, and the National Institute of Mental Health. The following is a brief list of some strategies you can try. Select ideas that seem most comfortable for you, try them for a while, and if they are not helpful, move on to the next one. Of course, if these techniques are not sufficient, please consider meeting with a licensed mental health professional for guidance and support.

1. **First, enlist self-compassion and kindness as you grapple with your anxiety.** As mentioned above, our species is wired to remain vigilant to anything that threatens our personal or family's well-being. Some of us are especially predisposed to heightened arousal and anxiety, whether due to genetics, biochemistry, past trauma, or even our own giftedness. We might find that we automatically experience an initial flash of frightening thoughts, startle easily, or harbor a tendency to think the worst. When this occurs, remind yourself that your heightened reactivity *also* graces you with profound empathy…or intensity…or compassion for others. We cannot change our innate predisposition; however, *we can learn* to manage our reactivity. Learning that we do not have to "obey" or automatically respond to our instinctive

reactivity is the first step. Notice these reactions and then remind yourself that you can choose a different course of action. Just like when you stub your toe—when it hurts like heck, but you know the pain will soon disappear—you can remind yourself that the intensity of your initial anxious response *will* subside once you guide your thoughts and feelings toward that goal.

2. **Engage your mind to quell your fears.** Based on the idea that emotions are influenced by underlying thoughts, assumptions and sometimes, distorted or negative thinking, cognitive-behavioral therapy (CBT) techniques[10-12] engage the logic underlying healthy choices. Often, we harbor irrational beliefs, false assumptions and "twisted" logic. For example, we might assume we know exactly what another person is thinking and suspect they are judging us. Or we might "catastrophize" and assume the worst possible outcome when our teen is out late. When we respond reflexively to these extreme beliefs, or "cognitive distortions," we may behave in a manner that creates further distress. The assumption underlying CBT is that negative thoughts trigger emotional distress, which then can lead to unhealthy responses, such as isolation, avoidance, defensiveness, or apathy. Rather than remaining chained to these unhealthy beliefs or behaviors, we can challenge ourselves to notice, question, and ultimately change our thoughts. As with other resources for managing anxiety, you can find a variety of articles, books and workbooks that explain CBT techniques. While it can be helpful to try these exercises on your own, you might find that a licensed mental health professional can guide you more effectively through this process.

3. **Practice mindfulness exercises.** Mindfulness is not just a meditation practice; it is an approach to daily life. When you attend to what you are experiencing at any given moment, you supersede the urge to ruminate about the past or worry about the future. You also get to enjoy the richness of life.

Who hasn't eaten snacks while watching TV and later realized they ate more than expected? Who hasn't multitasked while talking on the phone and then noticed that they lost track of the conversation? Mindfulness researchers have identified the core components of this practice: maintaining your attention on what you immediately experience in the moment and then cultivating "non-judgmental" acceptance toward the experience[14]. Research has indicated that the "default" mode for most of us is a "wandering mind," which contributes to a range of emotional, behavioral and physiological problems, including anxiety[15,16]. Our challenge involves retraining our brain to notice our thoughts without identifying *with* them or believing that they define us (for example, noticing the signs of anxiety, such as a clenched jaw or chest tightness without assuming that "I am an anxious person"). Brewer[17,18] and colleagues found that areas of the brain respond differently to anxiety-related thoughts among mindfulness practitioners. There is a wealth of online guidance, useful apps, and classes that support a mindfulness practice. Try out a variety of approaches until you find one that works for you.

4. **Speak with trusted friends and family about how they manage fears.** Anxiety often burdens us with feelings of shame and further isolation. Our culture and media confront us with images of fearless risk-takers, willing to tackle any challenge. Nevertheless, most people struggle with anxiety and fear at some point in time. As a species, we are hardwired to react when danger looms—even when others may not view the situation as threatening. When you reach out to people you trust, they can remind you of your strengths, share how they cope with their own fears, and offer support as you work on overcoming what upsets you. And reaching out sometimes normalizes our fears. As noted previously, parents of gifted children thrive when they can share their worries with other parents who understand and are experiencing the same struggles.

5. **Develop a list of supportive, calming strategies that will help to alleviate your anxiety.** Some people rely on daily exercise, meditation, or deep breathing techniques; others watch a comedy on TV, immerse themselves in a novel, or engage in a hobby or craft. Some discharge stress through creative activities, such as journaling, art, or dance. Most people benefit from supportive conversations with loved ones, even if reaching out can be tough at first. Imaginal rehearsal—where you calm your heightened physiological reactivity and then imagine calmly and successfully handling a potentially stressful situation—is a great tool for quelling fears. Pay attention to how your mood varies throughout the day, and notice what situations trigger greater distress, anger, or anxiety, and whether a confluence of events tips you over the edge. For example, you typically might feel resilient in the face of your child's tantrums, but need to take a break to calm yourself when you are exhausted or reeling from a stressful day at work. Appreciate your limits, the need for pacing yourself, and finding "rescue" strategies that will help calm you during times of stress. Everyone is different, and the more you learn about what works for you, the sooner you can implement these strategies.

6. **Practice preventative strategies.** Your stress-reduction toolkit should include an exercise routine, healthy eating, daily meditation or prayer, improving your sleep schedule, and finding time for joy in your life. Eliminate unhealthy behaviors, such as overeating, smoking or excessive alcohol use (and yes, that glass of wine can be a problem if you *must* have a drink every day). Prevention also includes planning ahead. This might involve seeking support and guidance ahead of an event or interaction that you suspect will cause some anxiety. It also means averting meltdowns or arguments with your child whenever possible. For example, you might avert disaster if you insist that your toddler stick with a nap schedule, keep snacks readily available, remove those scratchy

tags from the backs of clothing, or avoid restaurants with a long wait time.

7. **Consider seeking treatment with a licensed mental health professional.** Anxiety can be overwhelming at times. And while prevention, self-help strategies and support from family or friends are essential, sometimes additional guidance is needed. A recent review of the research literature[13] found that a combination of psychotherapy and medication is the most effective approach to managing anxiety. While the benefits of CBT were highlighted above, it should be noted that most psychotherapists combine a range of approaches (*not* just CBT) and use their experience and skills to find the best approach to address your concerns. Many people resist the idea of participating in psychotherapy or taking medication. Any hesitation is understandable when trying something new, or when sharing personal information about yourself with a treatment professional. If you are struggling with unrelenting anxiety, though, it is essential that you put aside any preconceived notions about psychotherapy. You will be helping yourself, as well as your child, who will reap the benefits of your calmer presence.

Identifying your anxiety and working on managing it will benefit both you and your child. When you use healthy coping strategies to overcome your worries, you also role-model a healthy response to anxiety. This includes conveying the value of support when you reach out to others. The more you compassionately understand and address your anxiety, the better you will feel, and the more clarity you will possess when making parenting decisions.

Regret and Guilt

Regret affects all of us; it is a universally experienced emotion. We regret what could have been, what we feel responsible for, and choices that went awry. Greenberg[19] defines regret as "a negative cognitive or emotional state that involves blaming ourselves for a bad outcome, feeling a sense of loss or sorrow at what might have been, or wishing we could undo a previous choice that we made." Most of us cope with small regrets without too much difficulty: not studying enough for an exam, purchasing the wrong brand at the store, or putting off returning a friend's phone call. The bigger regrets, though, are what catch in our throats and torment us: turning down a job that might have been ideal, not spending enough time with an ailing grandparent, betraying someone in a romantic relationship. These deeper regrets tap into feelings of guilt and shame. We blame ourselves and question our sense of self. *Why did I make that decision? Why didn't I know better?* When we struggle with regrets, it may be difficult to cultivate self-compassion and the acceptance that we are human and bound to make mistakes.

Regret also is a function of opportunities. When the future seems wide open, we juggle an array of choices. While this experience of "free will" may seem desirable, it carries the burden of responsibility and the potential for risk. Connelly and Zeelenberg[20] identified two core components of regret related to decision-making—a comparative assessment of the outcome of that decision and blaming ourselves for what seems like a bad choice. Belke and colleagues[21] have argued that "lost opportunities"—outcomes from the past that cannot be changed—stimulate the greatest feelings of regret, particularly when there is little sense of emotional closure related to the decision. It is not surprising that parents of gifted children may regret some of their decisions, especially given the array of possible directions available to their child, and the potential for guilt and anxiety associated with those lost opportunities.

> *Kendra and Kevin argued about how much to push their child academically. Kendra wanted to set stricter guidelines, but Kevin wanted their son, Jason, to "just be a kid." They agreed to allow Jason to make his own decisions when it came to high school classes and outside activities. Jason was bored with the easier classes he selected and spent his free time with friends playing video games. Jason's choices for college were more limited due to his lackluster school performance. He enrolled at a local branch of a state college and continued along a path*

of disinterest and minimal effort. Despite their earlier decision to allow Jason to set the pace, they both now regret backing down when it came to conveying clearer expectations. They worry that he may never regain his spark or his love of learning.

Parents of gifted children are quite aware of their child's potential. This infuses routine decisions with the prospect of regret: choosing a day care center with more convenient hours rather than one that provides greater enrichment, insisting that your child transfer to a more rigorous high school even though they must leave friends behind, wondering whether you should have supervised your child's oboe practice more, not saving enough for college. A gifted child's potential sometimes feels like a precious object that could be crushed at any time without vigilance and care. When we feel responsible for our child's health, happiness, academic success, and emotional adjustment, it is easy to second-guess our decisions. Roese and Summerville[22], for example, conducted a meta-analysis where they summarized the available research on regret. Parenting regrets were listed among the top four areas of concern, along with education, romance, and career. Regret was most likely to arise when faced with the greatest number of choices. The researchers concluded that the "biggest regrets are a reflection of where in life they see their largest opportunities; that is, where they see tangible prospects for change, growth, and renewal" (p. 1273). When your gifted child's future path is so full of possibilities, it leaves you primed to both question and potentially regret your decisions.

Powerful emotions can accompany regret. Seltzer[23], for example noted that regret "also encompasses *another* emotion—whether that's self-directed anger, embarrassment, humiliation, sorrow, depression, grief, guilt, shame, or remorse—or even some combination of these distressful emotions." In other words, regret can trigger a cascade of difficult and troubling emotions, or defenses against these emotions, such as denial or avoidance. Several researchers[24,25] also found a relationship between intense life regrets and changes in immune functioning, such as cold symptoms or effects on morning cortisol levels, which are associated with stress. Regret differs from disappointment, though; it is not tied to our personal sense of responsibility for the outcome of an event. As noted in Chapter 6, we may feel disappointed that our gifted child did not win an award we believe they deserved; however, we do not assume responsibility for this outcome. Zeelenberg and colleagues[26] distinguish regret from disappointment, noting that "regret is felt when one feels responsibility for an unwanted outcome, and disappointment is felt when outcomes fail to live up to expectations" (p. 224).

A close cousin of regret is guilt. As mentioned in Chapter 6, guilt differs from shame in that it typically arises after we behave in a manner that conflicts with our values and contrasts with how we typically view ourselves. Regret can lead to guilt, as we blame ourselves for our thoughts, feelings, actions, or inaction. Guilt arises after the fact when we realize we behaved in a manner that lacked integrity, was irresponsible, or was inconsistent with our values. It also occurs when our choices were hurtful to others or led to a negative outcome. For example, parents may feel guilt over their decision to keep their child in a school that refuses to address their academic needs.

> *Jake felt guilty about taking a job in another state and moving the family, just when his children were hitting their stride at school. They had a close group of friends, and the school provided a comprehensive gifted education program. Jake knew the job would pay well and would be challenging for him, yet he felt guilty about uprooting his family. He tried to remind himself that they would adjust but berated himself for his "selfish" career interests.*

Jake's ambivalence and guilt are typical for parents who hold high expectations for themselves and feel guilty when making a choice that benefits their own interests. It can be difficult to accept that we cannot always offer our children what they might want or need academically or interpersonally. Many parents of gifted children also experience "guilty thoughts" related to frustration or embarrassment over their child's behavior or their envy toward others. Yet, those who feel the most guilt often have less to feel guilty about, as their strong moral compass, perfectionism, or high expectations drive them toward intense self-scrutiny and a negative assessment of their actions. When we expect to have control over situations or always make the best decision possible, it is commonplace to lapse into self-blame. Many people who tend to feel guilty a lot also struggle with anxiety. Some of the suggestions listed in the previous section about anxiety may help with guilt and aid toward cultivating self-compassion and challenging excessively high expectations. Nevertheless, if your "guilty" actions are truly regrettable, you can learn from experience, plan to act differently next time, and apologize to those who might have been hurt.

Many parents of gifted children feel guilt related to their inability to effect change in the schools. Hackney[27] reported that parents of gifted children are frequently burdened by guilt and fear, along with feeling a strong sense of responsibility to help their children reach their potential. In the Gifted Parenting Survey, 71.3% of parents indicated that they "always" or "often" felt a daunting level of responsibility for guiding their child toward the best educational path. One parent relayed her feelings of guilt: *"I feel ill-equipped to provide her with the enrichment experiences she needs, and that stirs up guilt and shame."* This reaction is typical among many parents of gifted children; they blame themselves for not doing enough, even though they are not responsible for what occurs in the schools. And many parents lack the resources or inclination to homeschool or pay for private school or after-school activities. Sometimes anger turns to hopelessness and self-blame as some parents assume more than their share of responsibility. As another parent in the Gifted Parenting Survey commented:

> *"In hindsight, I wish we had more resources and sources to help us navigate. We feel a lot of guilt for her present situation—college graduate from a well-known college but struggling working piecemeal jobs that change every year. If she were happy, I'm sure I'd feel differently."*

How to cope with the "what-ifs" and "if only" questions that fuel guilt and regret

1. **Try to adopt a philosophical perspective about decision-making.** We typically make the best possible decision available to us at any given time. Who hasn't wished that our adolescent self had the wisdom and clarity we now possess? Who hasn't kicked themselves for turning down an opportunity that might have opened doors for their career? Even if we cringe over our choices, we can accept that we did not have the wisdom, experience, or foresight to handle the situation differently. As parents, we do the best we can, given our resources. We can learn from our regrets and plan to make changes going forward.

2. **Try to focus on the present.** You are responsible for your behavior *now* and cannot change what happened in the past. Try to forgive yourself for choices or behaviors you regret; we are only human, and we *all* make mistakes. When we feel shame over our actions associated with big regrets (e.g., driving while intoxicated, dropping out of high school, not always protecting our child from harm), we benefit from facing our guilt or shame, making amends, and learning how to behave differently going forward. Most regrets are not life-altering, though, and can be understood as actions taken with the best of intentions at the time.

3. **Consider whether you are assuming too much responsibility for your actions.** If you regret that you did not push your gifted child more to achieve, for example, accept that pressuring them might not have worked anyway, and could have backfired by fueling rebellion and further underachievement. While we are entrusted with guiding our children throughout their development, we cannot control their immediate choices, no matter how frustrating, infuriating, or disappointing. We can help by engaging in conversations about their behaviors, setting limits, changing expectations,

or sharing more about our values. But we are not solely responsible for their actions.

4. **Appreciate that regret can be a motivator.** It can encourage us to improve, learn, and try out new behaviors. It fosters humility and an acceptance that we make mistakes. Changing our attitudes and behaviors also models healthy self-awareness and flexibility for our children. If you regret yelling at your child, express your regrets once the dust settles. When we apologize for our actions, our children respect us even more. Regrets fester when we dig in our heels and refuse to learn from our past behaviors. While we cannot change what happened, working to understand how we would handle the situation differently shows that we can learn and grow from our mistakes.

5. **As mentioned in the section on anxiety, cultivating self-compassion and acceptance is essential.** When you experience regrets or feel guilt, evaluate your reactions. Determine whether your emotions are related to actions that warrant an apology and a change in your own behavior, or if they stem from harsh self-judgment and excessively high expectations. Sometimes, our guilt is justified. Sometimes, we are culpable. But even in those situations, compassionately acknowledging your fallibility and a willingness to change will assist you in moving forward. In other situations, though, your guilt may be excessive. Keep in mind that ruminating and berating yourself benefits neither you nor your child. Speaking with trusted friends, family, a licensed mental health therapist, or a member of your religious community can help with clarity and support.

A word or two about disappointment

Every parent suffers disappointment. Minor, common disappointments happen routinely, such as when your child repeatedly argues about chores or fails yet another exam. Larger and more distressing disappointments occur when your child endures rejection from a friend, fails an audition, or sits alone at home while other kids are at the prom. Much greater disappointment arises if your child lies to you about their alcohol use, suffers from serious mental health challenges, or drops out of school. Of course, while not all parents experience these more extreme examples of disappointment, any experience where your child suffers, loses out on much-desired opportunities, or behaves in a self-defeating or self-destructive manner can feel devastating.

As mentioned previously, disappointment differs from regret, as we typically do not assume personal responsibility or blame for what has occurred. We don't feel guilty or responsible; we just feel sad. Researchers Van Dijk and Zeelenberg[28] also distinguish between disappointment about an outcome or event and feeling disappointed in another person. They found that disappointment related to an event instilled a desire to try harder the next time or take a second chance, whereas disappointment in another person contributed to feelings of detachment and a desire to distance themselves from that individual. While the researchers did not study parental disappointment, their findings are nevertheless enlightening. As parents, our disappointment when our child is overlooked for an award or is not accepted to their first-choice college is quite different, for example, from distress over our child's behaviors or development. If we are disappointed in our child, we can feel sad, angry, disgusted, or embarrassed, and these emotions might lead to disengaging emotionally from them. Children sense when their parents are angry or disappointed, and certainly when they have pulled away. Many adults in psychotherapy bemoan situations where they received "the cold treatment" from parents, which invoked feelings of panic, helplessness, and despair. Many also claim that worries about disappointing their parents contributed to people-pleasing, perfectionism, or anxiety.

Disappointment also differs from grief, as grief typically stems from a more extreme and irrevocable loss. Grief is a normal process we all must endure at some point, and we typically move through it—aware that it becomes less painful over time. Sometimes, disappointment feels like grief; if our child suffers a profound disappointment or disappoints us to an extreme, we may grieve over their personal loss—or for the innocent and untarnished child they once were. Disappointment springs from love and empathy for our child. We feel their pain and are saddened when they suffer or act in a manner that diminishes them.

Parents of gifted children also may face specific disappointments that differ from what most neurotypical families experience. As noted in Chapter 6, disappointment sometimes stems from embarrassment over our child's lagging social maturity and asynchronous development. We may shake our heads in disbelief when our intellectually gifted child behaves in a manner so far outside the norm: rude, uncensored challenges to their teacher's authority; impatient, bossy interactions with peers; indignant refusal to complete a homework assignment they deem pointless. While disappointing, these situations typically evoke a sigh and a shrug; we realize that our child thinks and develops differently, and although we can guide them and try to shape their behaviors, they are on their own path. Other times, disappointment stings, and we are filled with anger and sadness, when, for example, our underachieving gifted child squanders their potential, or we watch helplessly as they endure rejection and bullying. We feel for them, but also feel powerless when we cannot remedy the situation. And sometimes our involvement can make the problem worse. School personnel, for example, may handle complaints about bullying in a clumsy manner and reprimand children who hold power in their peer group. This can incite even more intense targeting toward your child.

When routine frustrations and disappointments arise, we must consider our expectations, the rhythm of daily life, and long-held beliefs about child-raising. Picture-perfect Hallmark families, where children always cooperate and unkind words are never spoken, do not exist. Consider placing your child's disappointing behaviors in perspective if their actions are occasional occurrences, such as forgetting their homework or misbehaving at their grandparents' home. More frequently occurring situations may be a reminder that more work is needed. Your child may require more structure, supervision, tools for managing emotions, or ongoing discussion about empathy, judgment, manners, and your family's expectations about acceptable behavior. As discussed in Chapter 5, parents of gifted children often hold high hopes, given such vast potential. Nevertheless, your child may be on their own uneven, circuitous path, and your job is to notice, monitor and sometimes challenge your own expectations. While we may wish for our child's happiness, success, and a willingness to harness their potential, we cannot "will" this vision into action.

Weathering deeper disappointment enlists every one of our coping skills: reaching out to loved ones and trusted friends for support, digging deep to find personal resources for managing our feelings and reactions, challenging expectations and assumptions, and, for some, seeking mental health or spiritual guidance. Recognize that disappointment is a part of life. If we did not care so deeply, we would not feel our child's pain. We might wish to erect defenses that insulate us from emotional pain, but ultimately, this would distance us from our child. Like with all challenges, we can learn from disappointment. We also role model healthy coping skills when our child observes our capacity to handle disappointments and challenging emotions. When we support our child to accept the normalcy of disappointments, the ups and downs of life, and the resilience-building growth derived from weathering these experiences, we support their ability to move forward confidently.

What's next

The next chapter will address general parenting concerns, strategies, and approaches, and how these can be tailored to address behaviors associated with giftedness. All of us need a solid foundation and roadmap for our parenting decisions which can help us remain grounded even when we feel stressed and overwhelmed. Developing these skills and feeling secure in your parenting philosophy also can help with the many emotions discussed here and in previous chapters of this book.

CHAPTER EIGHT

Guidelines for Raising Your Gifted Child: The Importance of Love and Limits

Like all parents, we are tasked with setting a course of action for our children as we see fit. We might try to base parenting decisions on deeply held values, beliefs, and goals. However, real life gets in the way, and day-to-day parenting is frequently lacking such clarity and purpose. Many times, decisions are based on expediency or exhaustion. How many of us vowed never to plant our kids in front of the TV when life was hectic or swore that we would never yell at our kids—yet encountered a much different reality once we became parents? Other times, our choices are rooted in fears, insecurity, or unresolved conflicts from our family of origin. Despite our best of intentions, sometimes we relent and sidestep our values or standards.

Parenting gifted children intensifies these challenges. Daily, weekly, and even long-term decisions are infused with a level of uncertainty, as we grapple with our child's unique needs. Whether debating where they should attend school, or even planning for college, we must account for their thirst for knowledge, and also their intensity, heightened reactivity, asynchronous development, or anguish when the world seems unfair. Their glaring potential looms large; we weigh the relative importance of developmental and social/emotional needs with what might nurture their talents and pave a future path. As noted in previous chapters, we also must reckon with our own personal emotions and values to ensure that we make the best possible decisions for our child. Quite a tall order.

Many parenting philosophies circulate through popular media and often within your own network of family and community; in fact, you most likely have fielded more suggestions than you ever wanted! Family, friends, teachers, pediatricians, faith-based leaders, and even babysitters all have something to say. Parenting practices are passed down from each generation. Thousands of books and articles highlight child-raising theories, well-worn doctrine, or the latest trends. Like any parent trying to do their best, you might feel overwhelmed when presented with so many approaches.

Any parenting advice—including what I am suggesting here—must be weighed against your own personal values, your family's needs, and what is manageable at any given time. So, consider the guidelines in this chapter, mull them over a bit, and see what fits—*and* what does not. Although it may seem like you are winging it at times, the following basic tenets of "good enough parenting" can serve as general guidelines and provide clarity to help you stay on track, even on those chaotic and certainly imperfect parenting days. A basic framework includes loving support, providing a safe and trusting family environment, and setting appropriate limits. These essential components of parenting—love and limits—will be considered within the context of both your child's giftedness and the stressors and emotional challenges you face as the parent of a gifted child.

Love, empathy, and trust

Most parents would agree that expressing love for their child comes automatically. Yet, the devil is in the details. Daily challenges, your child's sometimes difficult behavior (at times, inflexible, demanding, whining, or oppositional), and your own personal stressors can temporarily sideline those loving feelings! Sometimes we are disappointed and angry, wish they would behave differently, or cringe when they fail to live up to expectations. While our love never wanes, sometimes we might not always *like* our child—or at least their behaviors. We are not always going to feel appreciative or grateful or have the energy to offer our loving attention. Momentary lapses from joyfully appreciating our child are normal and understandable. We are tasked though, with finding the strength to endure frustrations, disappointments, and troubling emotions, and to ground ourselves in an understanding of the importance of empathy and trust. And as mentioned throughout this book, we parent best when we understand our own motives and emotions.

The parent-child bond rests on a secure attachment. Children need to feel they are understood, and that you are attuned to the rhythms and fluctuations of their moods. Sharing a belly laugh with your toddler, calming your frightened child after a nightmare, knowing when to offer your prickly teen a hug—all typify an attuned and sometimes spontaneous, empathetic response to your child. Winnicott[1] described the importance of healthy "mirroring" with infants, where the parent's gaze and responsiveness accurately reflect what the child is experiencing. He emphasized that infants feel safe when they look at the parent and see their own emotional state reflected in the parent's face. Most parents automatically respond to their baby's emotions, for example, by smiling broadly when the baby coos and giggles, or frowning in response to their cries and exclaiming that the baby is upset. A parent's overall consistency with mirroring is significant; most infants overlook the parent's occasional distracted mood if they feel understood most of the time. However, disruptions can arise when a parent is chronically distracted, depressed, anxious, or angry, and often unable to respond in an attuned manner. In these situations, the infant can feel confused and anxious—sometimes expressing this through irritability and crying, and other times through apathy and withdrawal.

Attunement requires that we empathize with our child's feelings, but sometimes refrain from joining in. When your five-year-old's rage seems out of control, they are soothed by your calm and clear response, not by escalating to their level of intensity. Attunement and empathy sometimes demand restraint on your part; you might want to scream back at your angry child, but they will feel even more misunderstood—and possibly frightened that you seem as out of control as they feel. Attunement can be spontaneous at times, but also requires an overriding understanding of what your child needs at any given moment. Sometimes that means swallowing your own anger or anxiety or disappointment and helping your child navigate difficult emotions. *Honey, I know you are super mad about having to leave your friend's house, but it's not okay to try to hit me. It's time to sit quietly, hug your teddy bear, and take some slow deep breaths. I know you'll feel better in a little while.*

As children mature, they are better able to tolerate lapses in attuned attention. They recognize that parents get distracted and stressed— and sometimes even realize that you have a life of your own that is separate from them! However, the sense that you still "get them" and understand their feelings is essential—even when you don't always approve of their behavior or agree with their ideas. They may bemoan and resist the limitations placed upon them but will not doubt your love. Gifted children can be especially adept at pushing your buttons, debating you like a junior attorney, and blasting you with emotional outbursts. Children understand that parents are never thrilled with their oppositional behaviors; what is problematic, though, is when they assume that your love for them is in jeopardy. This might occur if your child views these disruptions in your affection as a withdrawal of your love, particularly if combined with angry outbursts, if you pull away emotionally, or if you express your disappointments by shaming them. It is completely normal and understandable to be angry or disappointed; however, it must be expressed whenever possible without rage or disgust. Even if your periodic lapses from loving and attuned attention seem like a reasonable response to a tough situation, your highly sensitive gifted child may question whether your love for them is fading.

What buffers children from these momentary lapses in attuned attention is the stability inherent in a mutually respectful, caring, flexible, and well-intentioned family environment. Frequent, enthusiastic, and affectionate expressions of love for your child—just for being who they are—is essential. Letting them know you love them, enjoy time with them, appreciate their unique, adorable, and amazing traits, and relish watching them grow and flourish, will create a sense of security they will carry into adulthood. For example, Olszewski-Kubilius and colleagues[2] conducted a survey of 1500 gifted students and their parents and reported findings that were "consistent with previous research in that affectionate, supportive, and respectful family environments appear to be important to the development of interpersonal skills and competency and peer relationships for gifted individuals" (p. 199). We cannot prevent some of life's mishaps and tragedies; however, we can provide a safety net through our loving, consistent, flexible, and attuned presence.

Much of parenting is a dance between attachment and letting go. And no one does this perfectly. We may hold on too tightly at times—perhaps fearful and grieving over our child's newfound independence, and hesitant to grant them the freedom they need. At other times, we may push them out the door too soon, intent on building their independence, and assuming that a "sink or swim" approach works best. Most of the time, though, we are seamlessly juggling these competing needs and making the best choice we can. *Should I let my five-year-old play at a new friend's home, even though I don't know the family very well? Should I speak with the teacher (once again) or expect my 10-year-old to advocate for himself? Do I trust my 13-year-old to go to the mall with her friends, without any adult supervision?* Such routine decisions draw on our strengths and values, but also underlying fears and insecurities. Understanding and acknowledging our uncertainties, worries, and even grief can provide greater clarity and a dose of self-compassion as we navigate this challenging territory.

A variety of approaches to parenting that emphasize warmth, acceptance and a respectful, collaborative parent-child relationship have expanded upon earlier concepts of attachment. Concepts such as positive parenting and approaches that emphasize creating safety in the parent-child relationship[3,4] suggest a shift from strict, authoritarian views of parenting. Seay[5] defined the concept of positive parenting, as "the continual relationship of a parent(s) and a child or children that includes caring, teaching, leading, communicating, and providing for the needs of a child consistently and unconditionally" (p. 207).

This approach has been associated with improved self-esteem, mental health, and school adjustment, and with fewer behavioral problems[6-9]. Rather than assuming we must control our child's actions, or rely on harsh dictates, we are asked to remain attuned to their emotional and developmental needs, and cultivate a flexible, caring, and empathetic response. This approach aspires to a collaborative and mutually respectful attitude toward problem-solving, and also takes a longitudinal perspective; parenting decisions are not merely based on resolving immediate problems, but are considered with the intention of building resilience, healthy decision-making abilities, and an appropriate level of responsibility in your child. It would follow that gifted children, with their heightened sensitivity, empathy, and insistence on fairness and justice, would be especially suited for such an approach.

Much has been written about the positive aspects of an authoritative parenting style. First proposed by Baumrind[10], three styles of parenting were identified based on the four dimensions of control, expectations, communication, and warmth.

1. Authoritarian parenting combines a high level of control and high expectations with lower levels of warmth and communication. This style is common among families who insist on rules, discipline and "no coddling." The motto "my way or the highway" fits their views. And while firm limits are certainly necessary at times, this approach may backfire, particularly with gifted children. A literature review[11] of the three parenting styles found higher levels of conduct problems, frustration, and insecurity, and lower levels of social competence among children of authoritarian parents.

2. Permissive parenting combines minimal control and few rules or expectations with greater levels of communication and warmth. The absence of clear rules and structure creates a level of instability, and children raised in permissive families may feel loved and appreciated, but exhibit more signs of social withdrawal, anxiety, or depression.

3. Authoritative parenting combines both of the above styles. There is a flexible level of control, where rules and standards are present, but children can offer their input and participate in some decisions. Authoritative parents hold high expectations, but they encourage independent thinking. There are high levels of communication and warmth, and children raised in authoritative families typically exhibit healthy social and coping skills, a secure attachment style, and a positive self-concept.

Not surprisingly, an authoritative style, as proposed by Baumrind[10], may be the most effective parenting style for raising gifted children. Eager to parse through every directive, frequently willing to debate you over any request, and reluctant to follow rules without some input, gifted children quickly balk at authoritarian directives. It just doesn't make sense to them. Dwairy[12], for example, found that "parents of gifted adolescents tend to be more authoritative and less authoritarian than parents of nongifted adolescents. The authoritative parental style correlates positively with the mental health of both gifted and nongifted adolescents, while the authoritarian parenting style impacts negatively on the mental health of the gifted, but not of the nongifted adolescents. The study results indicate that the authoritarian parenting style is a crucial factor that influences the well-being of gifted children and may affect their psychological adjustment" (p. 275).

Academic achievement also has been linked to parenting style. Dornbusch and colleagues[13] reported a correlation between authoritative parenting and a gifted child's level of achievement and good grades, and that both authoritarian and permissive parenting styles were negatively associated with grades. Interestingly, children from inconsistent families, who combined authoritarian with other parenting styles, had the lowest grades. Huey[14] and colleagues also found an association between authoritative parenting styles and an increase in grades among gifted students who were early college entrants.

Authoritative parenting has been associated with higher cognitive performance in adolescents and with their secure attachment as adults[15]. Some reports comparing parents of gifted children to those with neurotypical children have found that parents of the gifted were more communicative and warm[16], and more expressive and less controlling[17]. They also were more likely to report unconditional love for their child, spent more time with them on school-related activities, and encouraged their independence[18]. Questions for future research might include identifying whether certain characteristics predispose parents of gifted children to adopt an authoritative parenting style, or whether parents of the gifted are merely responding to their gifted child's inherent need (demand!) for warmth, empathy, and a more communicative relationship.

Regardless of parenting style, most parents try to provide as secure and stable a home environment as possible. A stable environment is not necessarily trouble-free, though. Every family experiences stress, disappointments, conflict, and setbacks, especially during times of financial hardship, illness, or loss. These situations provide an opportunity for you to role-model healthy coping strategies and good conflict-resolution skills. It also reminds your child that despite setbacks in the family, they are still loved, that you will protect them as much as possible, and that you trust their strength and resilience to weather difficult situations.

How do we create stability and security? The following are some basic guidelines to consider:

1. **Convey acceptance for your child's feelings or reactions, even if you disagree or think they are overreacting.** Let them know that you understand their distress, *and* that you also trust their resilience and ability to move past their disappointments. Create an expectation that all emotions are acceptable, even if certain behaviors are not. Anger is an understandable feeling that arises when a child feels wounded; hitting their brother in response to anger is not an acceptable behavior. Insist on a family environment where tears are never mocked or criticized, feelings and opinions are never shamed, and where any topic is open for discussion.

2. **Let them know that you can handle their feelings.** When children sense that a parent becomes easily overwhelmed or enraged, they will keep their feelings hidden. Children feel more secure when they do not have to worry about your anger, anxiety, or distress. In essence, you are there to take care of them—*not* the reverse. And if you would like your adolescent to confide in you or call you when a party gets out of hand, building a trusting relationship early on is essential. Children who claim that a parent is their "best friend" often view their parent as an equal. While this might seem positive, it often implies a relational dynamic where the child cannot rely on the parent, or feels they must bolster the parent's self-esteem. We want our children to respect and consider our feelings; however, they also need to believe that we are strong and have no need for them to worry about us.

3. **Role-model healthy conflict resolution skills, respect for others, and healthy coping strategies.** Demonstrate honesty, trust, direct communications, and healthy conflict-resolution through your actions, and especially in your relationship with your partner or spouse, friends, and extended family members. If you respond harshly to someone—or making critical or prejudicial comments behind their back—your child may assume you feel that way toward them also. Respond honestly to their questions within reason; you can refuse to share information that is private or that might be hurtful to them. For example, they do not need to know the specifics of your financial affairs or a detailed account of your adolescent escapades. You can let them know that for a variety of reasons, you are not ready to answer a particular question.

4. **Respect their developmental level.** When you expect too much or too little from your child, you disregard their capabilities. A gifted child's developmental level, though, can be hard to pin down when asynchronous development clouds the picture. Your eight-year-old may delve into research like

a junior scientist yet lack the confidence and social skills to interact with same-age cousins at a family gathering. Target your expectations to their developmental level and skills, and always convey your belief that they are resilient and capable.

5. As mentioned in previous chapters, **pay attention to your own reactions, emotions, and needs.** You are better equipped to respond to your child's needs with calm and clarity if you understand the origins of your motivations and feelings and how your extended family, the community, and current trends have influenced you. This requires a willingness on your part to explore your past and recognize what influences your parenting decisions. If you find yourself responding impulsively or with excessive anger, it is time to take stock and work on managing your reactions. If you withdraw from your child, respond to them with heightened anxiety, or feel hopeless, it is time to find parenting support. As Siegel and Hartzell[19] have noted:

> Research in the field of child development has demonstrated that a child's security of attachment to parents is very strongly connected to the parents' understanding of their own early life experiences... If you had a difficult childhood but have come to make sense of those experiences, you are not bound to recreate the same negative interactions with your own children. Without such self-understanding, however, science has shown that history will likely repeat itself, as negative patterns of family interactions are passed down through the generations (p. 15).

Ultimately, we want our children to feel good about themselves, but also develop resilience, learn to manage their emotions, and become well-functioning adults. Learning to identify and accept their needs and differences is essential. Developing tools for coping with strong emotions, such as finding outlets for appropriate expressions of anger, or calming strategies for anxiety, is also necessary. The more (albeit imperfect) attunement, safety, and calm guidance we provide, the more likely they will feel confident as they mature.

Discipline and limit-setting

Gifted children can present quite a challenge when it comes to discipline. Whether throwing a tantrum mid-aisle at the grocery store, or questioning your rules with legalistic flair, your gifted child is no stranger to intensity…or conflict…or pushing the limits. It may be difficult to coax them to comply when they believe the task is just plain *wrong*; if expectations seem unfair, unnecessary, too difficult, too easy, poorly conceived, wasteful, or an affront to their values, they will resist. Gifted children expect logic, honesty, and compassion, even in response to their misbehavior; anything less will evoke their distrust and feelings of betrayal. They assume that the adults in charge will be reasonable and kind, but like most children, may not grasp that parents are sometimes stressed to the max, or behave inconsistently, or are not necessarily calm when doling out discipline. Most gifted children understand that a "time-out" or loss of a favorite toy is warranted in response to unacceptable behavior—even if they don't like the consequences. If the punishment seems out of proportion to the transgression, though, they will resent it. And despite their expectation that *you* must behave logically, they may respond with limited rationality: angry tirades, tantrums, emotional outbursts, and rigidity are common reactions.

Just about every parent struggles at some point with limit-setting or discipline. Children thrive in a loving environment that also includes clear, consistent, and reasonable limits. This creates a feeling of safety and predictability. Nevertheless, children frequently resist expectations and demands and wish they had more autonomy, even while they simultaneously realize that some rules are necessary. Whether through spunk, strategy or manipulation, most kids will push the limits when they detect an opportunity, especially if we have been inconsistent in the past. The concept of intermittent reinforcement highlights this dilemma for us as parents; whether due to exhaustion, distraction, or a loving gesture of spontaneous generosity, when we diverge from our typically consistent ground rules, we unleash our child's determined persistence the next time they want something from us. In other words, they suspect that with just enough pleading, whining, or arguing, we might give in. You may have purchased that candy bar *just this one time* because the check-out line was exceptionally long, and you wanted to avert a melt-down. However, your child might interpret the situation differently, tuck that information away, and assume that maybe next time, if they complain loudly enough, they can get their way. Kurcinka[20], for example, has written about "spirited children;" highly intense, persistent, energetic, and sensitive—something most parents of gifted and twice-exceptional children know quite well! These are kids who just do not back down—at least not until they grasp your rationale or realize that you are sticking with your decisions. Conflicts can arise when there is some room for debate, as with homework, bedtime, screen time, grades, time with friends, purchases, chores, and dating. As parents, it helps to consider expectations with an understanding of your child's developmental level and temperament, the values you wish to instill, and the goal of keeping your family functioning as smoothly as possible. As much as they may resist, most children understand the rationale for a consistent bedtime, for example, or arriving at school on time. And some expectations are accepted as non-negotiable, such as buckling their seatbelt. Each child is different, though, and may struggle with even the most basic expectations or rules.

Consistency also adds to the safety and structure children need. Parenting with consistency assumes some level of agreement between the adults in the household. When children sense that their parents disagree about rules and limits, they will use that to their advantage and even attempt to play one parent against the other. Of course, you and your spouse or partner are not always going to agree. What is critical is finding time (*out of earshot* from your child) where you can discuss what is most important and determine when to compromise. It is equally essential to avoid criticizing your spouse or partner in front of your child. Certainly, you must intervene if your partner or spouse is behaving erratically or there is a threat of violence. Otherwise, disagreements should be handled when your child is not present. Consistency also is upheld when your child knows what to expect, can anticipate how you will respond to certain infractions, and sees that you treat siblings equally; if your child suspects favoritism or unfair treatment toward any child in the family, you may risk losing their trust.

Your flexibility also demonstrates to your child that you weigh and measure each situation and sometimes may change the rules accordingly, while remaining grounded in your overriding principles. Your child may know that bedtime is at 9:00, but also appreciate that permission to stay up later happens when relatives are visiting. Your child will understand that allowing them to overlook their chores after an upsetting incident at school is an extension of your kindness, not a sign that rules will change in the future. Although gifted children are adept at detecting opportunities to debate rule changes, their intellectual abilities allow for a nuanced understanding of changing family routines. Your flexibility also conveys a willingness to sometimes "break the rules" and veer from routine to enjoy time with your child; an unexpected excursion to the beach, a trip to the ice cream store, a rainy day spent playing board games—all show your child how much you delight in spending time with them.

The best form of punishment is one that never needs to be used. You and your child are both well-served when you can predict and prevent situations that lead to conflict. Gifted children may become easily overstimulated…or become bored and act up to amuse themselves… or overthink and worry about a new situation, resulting in a balky refusal to participate. Anticipating and then avoiding situations bound to cause chaos or distress is an advantage for all involved. For example, dragging your toddler to the store when they are hungry or missed their nap is a recipe for disaster. Some children respond best to incentives, where they work to achieve a goal or reward for accomplishing a task. Examples might include an extra hour of screen time for a week of not fighting with siblings, or extra allowance for consistently getting ready for school in the morning without an argument. Since these goals are determined in advance, they differ from bribes and can be reviewed and revised over time. Develop a sense of when to push and when to let go of your own expectations. Through a better understanding of what triggers your child's reactions, along with a fair and reasoned approach to limits and discipline, your gifted child will recognize that certain problem behaviors will not accomplish what they want.

Preventing misbehavior is ideal, although not always possible or realistic. When prevention fails, you need sound principles that will guide you through some tough choices. Many times, though, families rely on well-worn advice, tactics drawn from how they were raised, or practices based on expediency rather than a meaningful consideration of what your child needs. Clearly, some strategies are less effective than others, and could be traumatic for your child. Treating one sibling much differently, doling out an extreme and harsh punishment, name-calling, shaming, or spanking are problematic for any child— but gifted children will view your actions as irrational and unjust, and may build a wall of resentment. Worse still, they may internalize harsh words and believe that they are intrinsically "bad," or become fearful and resolve to keep their feelings to themselves.

Any form of physical punishment must be avoided. Even if you were spanked as a child and believe you turned out just fine, there is abundant evidence pointing to the detrimental effects of physical punishment[21,22]. Even if you convince yourself that spanking is a controlled, dispassionate form of discipline, you may be angrier than you think. And children pick up on that. They will sense your anger, which is transmitted along with the sting of the slap. You would not hit your neighbor, spouse, or co-worker. Why is it acceptable, then, to hit a child who is half your size? Sensitive gifted children, in partic-ular, feel terrified when the parent they love towers over them with hands raised. Gifted children typically cannot "shake off" what they view as an assault. Their active minds also process this experience as unjust and harsh, and they may retreat, distrust, and lose respect for you. A wealth of research highlights the relative ineffectiveness and detrimental effects of physical punishment[23-25], and numerous orga-nizations, such as the American Academy of Pediatrics, the American

Psychological Association, and the United Nations Committee on the Rights of the Child have condemned this practice.

Nelson[4] has suggested that unintended consequences ensue when harsh disciplinary measures are used. He highlighted what he referred to as the "four R's"—rebellion, resentment, revenge, or retreat—as reactions to harsh discipline. It makes sense that sensitive gifted children who feel unfairly and harshly treated or who endure verbal assaults will enlist defense mechanisms to protect themselves from future hurt. If your spouse, friend, or employer mocked you, treated you with disdain, or screamed at you, it is likely that you would feel angry or fearful of future conflicts. However, children do not possess the same freedom as adults, who have the option to leave a marriage, friendship, or job; they are dependent on you and have few options for escape. Webb and colleagues[26] also cautioned against the use of sarcasm or ridicule, which is hurtful to a sensitive gifted child. They urged parents to avoid harsh punishment of any kind, which they defined as: "not only physical punishment like spanking, but also angry shouting and verbal, emotional or other abuse—in short, any punishment that is inappropriate, over the top, or does not fit the crime" (p. 114). Disciplinary practices that enlist positive discipline[4], an attitude of compassion and empathy when addressing behavioral problems[3], and a collaborative and proactive solutions approach[27], are useful frameworks for addressing problem behaviors. These approaches all emphasize the importance of direct communication with your child, using misbehavior as an opportunity for teaching new skills, cultivating empathy for your child's experience, and remaining attuned to their developmental and emotional needs. Using these values as a framework for handling misbehavior will guide you at times of heightened emotion.

What should you consider when your gifted child needs more than structure or limits and requires some form of discipline?

1. **Consider your child's mindset.** What was your child's motivation when committing the offensive act? Was it planned, impulsive, hurtful to others, manipulative, deceptive, or an

attempt to grab your attention? Was it an understandable response to a tough situation, or completely out of line? Does your child possess the impulse control or decision-making and social skills to make better choices the next time? What is appropriate for your child's developmental level? Assessing your child's motivations, capabilities, maturity, and the situation at hand will help you formulate a plan.

2. **Consider *your* mindset.** Are you paying attention to *how* you address infractions with your child? Are you anticipating the long-term impact of your disciplinary choices? Webb and colleagues[26] have proposed considering the following three factors when disciplining gifted children: the effectiveness of your approach *in the long run*, its impact on your child's self-esteem, and its effect on your relationship with your child. Discipline that demands immediate compliance may not hold up over time and even may erode trust. Any disciplinary approach must consider a longitudinal perspective; parenting decisions should not merely focus on resolving the immediate problem, but guide your child in the process of building resilience, healthy decision-making, and an appropriate level of responsibility. Such a balanced perspective enlists understanding and compassion—an attitude your child will sense and appreciate.

3. **Consider your approach.** Do you pay attention to your tone of voice when you express anger? Do you appreciate that how you handle conflicts may be particularly distressing to an emotionally sensitive child? Is your discipline consistent with a commitment to convey loving, warm, and trusting acceptance—even in the midst of conflict? You may be furious, but as an adult, can choose to express your frustration without hurtful, shaming accusations, or generalizations which imply that your child is "bad." Does your discipline or punishment seem logical; does it make sense to your child, even if they disagree or complain about it? Gifted children appreciate logic, even if they do not agree with

the outcome. Enlist the strength of their logical thinking to help them understand the rationale behind decisions. Of course, this does not mean debating for hours; instead, point out your reasoning, let them respond, and then insist that they move on. Very young children and toddlers may not respond to skills-building or logic, though. Ramsburg[28] has suggested some strategies parents can use to halt problem behaviors in young children, such as clapping your hands loudly to get their attention, or crouching down to their level, and speaking calmly and firmly. There are many excellent books[3,4,19,26,27,29] that describe specific child-raising and disciplinary strategies. Consider researching what you feel might work best for you and your child.

4. **Consider your child's skillset.** What skills does your child need to develop? Rather than trying to correct your child's oppositional behavior, Greene[27] has suggested viewing the behavior as a signal that your child is struggling, cannot meet expectations, or lacks sufficient skills to manage their emotions. Your job is to problem-solve, rather than focusing solely on modifying your child's behavior. When you are enraged, you are more likely to view your child negatively—as "bad," manipulative, or oppositional. You may feel less anger if you can compassionately consider that your child may possess deficits in the skills necessary for healthy choices. For example, Greene's "collaborative and proactive solutions" model proposes that children misbehave because they lack at least one of the following: executive functioning skills, social skills, cognitive flexibility, emotional regulation skills, or the ability to clearly communicate their needs.. Everyone gets angry. Your child needs you to provide guidance related to *how* they can manage these feelings. For example, a young child can be guided to punch a pillow or discharge energy by running around the yard instead of hitting you. An older child can do the same, but also write a story or use art to express their feelings. All children benefit from learning deep

breathing and other calming techniques, as well as "using their words" to express their feelings.

5. **Consider what is working.** Do you acknowledge good behavior? When life is going well, it is easy to forget that all children appreciate recognition when they are behaving, complete expected tasks, and demonstrate mature, considerate, or helpful behaviors. The expression, *"catch them being good,"* still holds. The amount of praise or reward needs to fit the scope of the behavior. But even comments like, «hey, thanks for helping with the dishes,» or «it was great to see you and your brother playing quietly at your grandparent›s house» can have an impact. Excessive praise for the most minor task is unnecessary; just remember to let your child know how much you appreciate kindness, cooperation, patience, and responsible behavior.

6. **Consider what enhances learning and ongoing growth.** Is there a learning component inherent in any discipline? Is your child recognizing that their behaviors have consequences, that they have the power to assume responsibility for their actions, and that negative behaviors hurt others? Can they notice progress in their ability to contain their impulses or plan more effectively? Can you include them in decision-making? You might ask an older gifted child what they view as appropriate punishment for certain behaviors, along with meaningful incentives for completing tasks. If you agree with your child's suggestions, you could incorporate them into a plan for handling the next transgression. This level of participation gives your child a sense of control and involvement in the process and may enlist future cooperation.

7. **Consider creative solutions.** Can you devise creative solutions that might best meet your child's and your family's needs? This may appeal to your gifted child's logical mind and makes sense to them. Consider consequences that

require action on their part. Rather than using time-outs or removing a favorite object, you could require "community service" at home. Sending your child to their room, for example, may not seem like much of a burden, whereas requiring an activity that compensates for a transgression may have more of an impact, such as cleaning the kitchen or raking the lawn. Can you ask your child to make amends? If the transgression involved destruction of property or hurting someone's feelings, insist that your child generate a plan for making amends. A quick, empty apology is not enough. Ask them to come up with a more heartfelt expression of regret for their behavior in words or action, such as repairing the damaged item, saving up to purchase the toy that was broken, or expressing a heartfelt verbal apology. As much as your child may not like any of this, it will appeal to their logic and sense of fairness.

8. **Consider your self-awareness.** Are you aware of how experiences in your family of origin and in your primary relationships have affected your views related to parenting? Are your responses to your child driven by unresolved fears, anger, insecurity or even trauma? As noted throughout this book, remaining attentive to your own personal and emotional reactions, and working on resolving emotional distress will infuse parenting decisions with greater clarity. No more knee-jerk reactions that you might regret! And once you recognize and understand your fears and expectations, you can see your child more clearly, and their problem behaviors may not seem as insurmountable. As Siegel and Hartzell[19] have noted:

> "Your children give you the opportunity to grow and challenge you to examine issues left over from your own childhood…Having the attitude that you can learn throughout your life enables you to approach parenting with an open mind, as a journey of discovery" (p. 24).

What's next...for you?

As the parent of a gifted child, you may strive for the highest standards; yet nagging fears, insecurities, and entrenched patterns of behavior can derail your very best of intentions. It takes courage to question your attitudes, feelings, and behaviors, and to move forward with change. Regardless of whether tasked with daily parenting decisions or long-range goals, you also must consider your own needs. Parenting reminds us of our own childhood—what worked well and what went wrong. Some of our most difficult challenges occur when memories surface, or when our perceptions of our childhood experiences take on a different meaning. You also learn that every child, every family, and every situation are different; it is up to you to sort through the information available and tailor it to what your family needs.

Parenting a gifted child confers an added element of both of joy and stress. This book has highlighted some of the complexities inherent in giftedness and how this affects us as well. Despite the emphasis on difficulties and challenges, it is essential to appreciate the many wonderful, energizing, joyful experiences that arise. It can be helpful to pause and enlist gratitude for your child and your gifted parenting experience. Several comments from the Gifted Parenting Survey highlight these joys:

> *"While I worry a lot about the day to day—watching my child's brain engage and soar fills me with wonder and hope."*

> *"So many [challenges], but as a parent of a young adult who turned out great, I'd tell younger parents that it gets better."*

> *"It's not an easy journey; there's a lot of misinformation and misunderstanding. But I will never change the experience of raising a gifted kid."*

Nevertheless, as you juggle your child's intense social, emotional, and academic needs with their remarkable potential, you may question your decisions. When so many parenting choices are infused with this added pressure, and educators and community members remain oblivious to the impact of giftedness on a family, you can feel overwhelmed and alone. And while increased self-awareness may relieve you of some long-suppressed emotional burdens, you also may experience some distress when unexpected emotions or memories arise. These challenges highlight the necessity of finding support along the way. As noted previously, it is critical that you find supportive friends, family, and parents within the gifted community who will join with you as you navigate parenting challenges. And sometimes, seeking support from a licensed mental health professional can help you understand and express your emotional burdens and gain perspective. When you make a commitment to continued self-reflection, achieve a deeper and more compassionate understanding of yourself, and find close connections with others, you will acquire the clarity and confidence you need along this parenting journey.

Afterword

Parenting a gifted child can feel like a roller coaster ride full of joy and stressful challenges. As you balance your gifted child's intense social, emotional, and academic needs with their remarkable potential, you may question your decisions. When so many parenting choices are infused with this added pressure, and educators and community members remain oblivious to the impact of giftedness on the family, you can feel overwhelmed and alone. In some ways, "gifted" is still a dirty word; there is much work to be done to overcome widespread misunderstanding, stigma, and inequity. The reality that some children think differently is discounted; their neurodiversity, their thirst for knowledge, and their tendency to often (although not always) possess emotional intensities is rarely understood.

Parenting *any* child exposes us to our deepest wishes, vulnerabilities, and fears. It takes courage and persistence to face these head-on and appreciate the learning curve that comes with parenting. It also reminds us of our own childhood—what worked well and what went wrong. Some of the most difficult challenges arise when old memories surface, or when perceptions of childhood experiences take on a different meaning; when you become a parent, you gain an appreciation of the complexities involved in parenting that you never imagined. Your worldview is forever changed.

As a parent of two gifted children, I experienced the same ups and downs many of you face. It was a joy to watch them explore, grow, and develop into the kind and accomplished young men they are today. But there were many challenges along the way. Like most of you, I had worries and concerns. Even though I was trained as a psychologist, I still faced daily surprises and had much to learn. Finding the right academic fit, ensuring that their social needs were met, and college planning all presented unique challenges. And even though their public school education was limiting at times, I am grateful for the many wonderful teachers who went the extra mile to provide additional enrichment beyond what was typically available in the regular classroom. I was fortunate to join and eventually co-chair a gifted parents advocacy group, where we fought for district-wide changes in how the schools identified giftedness and implemented gifted education.

My own gifted parenting journey also allowed me to review my past experiences and assumptions. I was quite aware that I hoped to parent differently than what I experienced in my childhood; nevertheless, my parenting was far from perfect. I also revisited memories from my years in school. No stranger to boredom and underachievement in high school, I had formed long-held assumptions about my strengths, weaknesses and talents that persisted long after receiving my Ph.D. Parenting provides a wake-up call; it creates an uninvited, yet powerful opportunity to explore past assumptions and create new perspectives going forward.

Once my children graduated from high school, I wanted to remain involved with advocating for the needs of gifted children and their families. I continued my work with gifted adolescents, parents of gifted children, and adults in my psychotherapy practice, and offered consultations to help parents with decisions related to their gifted child's education and college trajectory. I created a blog, Gifted Challenges, which focused on the social/emotional, parenting, and advocacy issues familiar to families of the gifted. I also authored online and newsletter articles and several book chapters, and offered workshops to parenting groups and schools. I hope to continue my advocacy work to provide clarity and support for families of the gifted and to offset the persistent stereotypes and stigma associated with giftedness

This book has highlighted some of the complexities of giftedness, and how this affects parents of gifted children. Any challenges and difficulties, though, are offset by the many wonderful, energizing, joyful experiences that arise. It can be helpful to pause and feel gratitude for your child and your gifted parenting experience. As one parent in the Gifted Parenting Survey expressed, *"She's pretty amazing and I'm glad she's mine!"* Appreciating who your child is and relishing this exciting journey is a joy—and an antidote to those trying times.

I hope that this book has provided some additional insight and support as you navigate through your amazing gifted parenting journey. I wish you well as you continue to explore giftedness, understand your own personal history, and find joy in parenting your child. Your attuned awareness to your child's needs, a grounding in the core parenting values of love and limits, your ongoing self-reflection and willingness to challenge stubborn resistances and fears, and a willingness to seek camaraderie and support will guide you through this journey. Perfection is never required; a compassionate and open-minded perspective is all you need. Making a commitment to continued self-reflection, achieving a deeper and more compassionate understanding of yourself, and finding close connections with others will support you through this parenting journey—both now and after your gifted child has grown.

Results from the
Gifted Parenting Survey

Survey rationale and methodology

The Gifted Parenting Survey was designed to gather information about the gifted parenting experience from parents themselves. Although much of the information found in this book is grounded in theory, research, and clinical experiences, I also wanted to include direct input from parents of gifted children, teens, and young adults. The survey consisted of 24 questions that covered family demographics, information about their child's strengths and challenges, parents' reactions and concerns related to their child's experience, and how parenting a gifted child has affected them as parents. Some of these questions asked participants to select only one response from a series of options; others permitted responses to any or all of the items. The survey included an additional option where participants could share descriptions of their child or their own experience. Some of these comments have been included in the chapters of this book.

The survey was distributed online through the following: my professional website, gailpost.com; my blogsite, giftedchallenges.com; several social media sites such as Facebook and Twitter; several Facebook discussion groups dedicated to the gifted parenting experience; professional groups pertaining to giftedness; and other online groups dedicated to parenting gifted children. Participants were informed that their participation in the survey was optional, that results would remain confidential, and that results would be presented in this book and in additional articles. Participants reviewed the following request before proceeding with the survey:

> *"Please consider participating in a brief survey about your experience as a parent of a gifted child. I am so grateful that many of you continue to read my blog, Gifted Challenges! Now, I am asking for YOUR input. There is very little research currently on the lived experience of parenting a gifted child. The information gathered from this survey will be included in my upcoming book. In addition to the clinical and research information that will be included in the book, I hope to use these survey findings to enlighten and support other families on this journey. (Please feel free to participate in this survey even if your child is now a young adult.)*
>
> *Please note that all information obtained from this survey will remain confidential. If you choose to share personal examples in several of the sections below, use of this material will be disguised to obscure any identifying information. The survey should take approximately ten minutes to complete. If you would like to participate in a random drawing for a $50.00 Amazon gifted card, you will be asked to include your email so that I may contact you. Please note that I will not link your email to any of the answers you provide.*
>
> *By completing this survey, you are granting authorization for use of your responses in research related to giftedness. While this survey should not cause any harm, if you experience any level of distress related to questions in the survey, please feel free to contact me. Thank you."*

Results

Responses were collected over the span of six weeks in 2022. A total of 810 individuals visited the site and more than half completed the survey. Results were obtained from 428 participants who completed the survey, with a completion rate of 52.8%. It is not known why the remaining visitors did not complete the survey. Statistical analyses were not performed for the purpose of this book; rather, an over-view of demographic information, child characteristics, and parent opinions are summarized. Results are displayed through graphs on the following pages, and I have offered my comments about some of the findings. Demographics about the child, along with the child's school status, gifted identification, additional talents, and twice excep-tional issues are presented first. After that, parent demographics, the parent's observations about their child, and their personal reactions to parenting are presented.

Limitations

As you will see in the following pages, results were drawn mostly from parents who were White and who lived in the United States; as a result, survey data may not reflect the experiences of persons of color or those who live outside of the United States. Almost all of the responses came from women, and their opinions may not reflect what men think about their children or the parenting experience. A few of the "parents" in the study also noted that they are grandpar-ents raising their gifted grandchild. Some participants were parents of young adults; their responses were retrospective accounts, and while this provides both a broader, long-range perspective, their child's experience may not be reflective of what is currently offered in schools today. Many of the participants indicated that their child had not been formally evaluated (often due to their young age), but they suspected that their child was gifted based on precocious behaviors. Even among school-aged children, some were identified for gifted services based on classroom achievement tests or teacher selection. Finally, validated test measures were not used in this study. As a result, findings must be considered with the understanding that they are opinion-based and subjective. One parent's opinions about their child's behaviors, talents, and emotions may not be comparable to what another parent observes.

The greatest limitations of this survey stem from the use of a non-random sample; participants were recruited from online sites where parents of gifted children gather to acquire information, guidance, and support. As a result, findings may be skewed because most participants likely possess extensive knowledge about giftedness and gifted education, given their participation in social media sites designed to provide information and support. These families may differ from what might be found within a random sampling of families in a particular school district, for example. Nevertheless, information drawn from such a large sample provides a solid foundation for understanding what many parents observe and experience as they raise their gifted child. Further research is needed to understand more about the gifted parenting experience.

How to interpret these findings

As you review the data on the following pages, you may have strong reactions. Some of the findings may be validating and fit with your lived experience. Others may seem puzzling and unfamiliar. You might wonder why some of your personal reactions differ so much from those expressed by the majority of survey participants. Please keep in mind that findings from this survey include only a small segment of the gifted parenting population, and their experiences may differ from yours. However, your commitment to your gifted child's personal growth, academic potential, and emotional adjustment are values both you and the survey participants share in common. Please approach the data with a spirit of curiosity and an open mind.

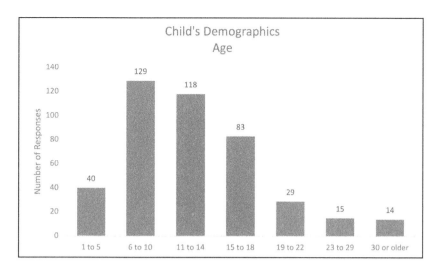

Participants were asked to identify only one child (if they have more than one gifted child) for the purpose of this survey. It should be noted that 66.2% of participants indicated that they have more than one child, and 52.3% of participants overall indicated that more than one child in their family is gifted or suspected to be gifted. A small proportion of children in this survey (13.5%) were 19 or older and no longer in elementary or secondary schools.

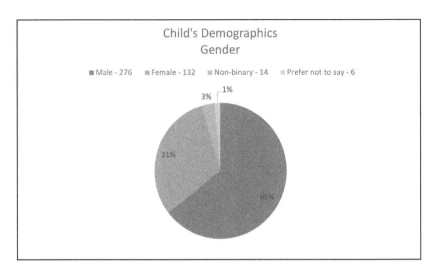

It is interesting that almost two-thirds of children described in this survey are male. Why are the majority of survey respondents parents of boys? One consideration includes possible characteristics of this sample. Questions for the survey were solicited through online and social media forums. Boys tend to have more difficulty adjusting to traditional classrooms and are more likely to present with twice exceptional conditions, such as ADHD, ASD, or learning disabilities. As a result, boys may struggle to adapt to the classroom setting, leading to increased family stress. The parents' level of distress and quest for solutions might contribute to a greater proportion of parents of boys who seek guidance within online communities (and possibly explain the much higher percentage of parents of boys who were available to participate in this survey). Further research would be needed to clarify why a higher proportion of families of boys participated in this study.

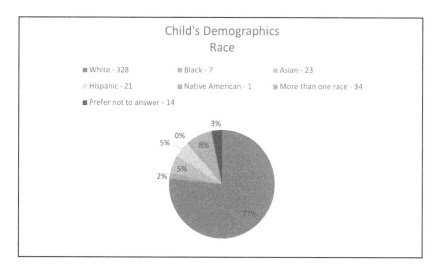

As seen in this graph, a large portion of participants indicated that their child is White. As a result, data from the survey may not be representative of what gifted persons of color experience.

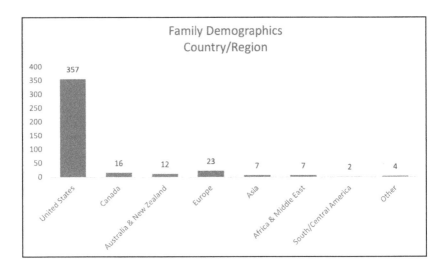

Survey responses were skewed heavily toward U.S. residents (83.4%). While responses provide useful information about parenting gifted children in the U.S., results may not be reflective of parenting concerns in other countries.

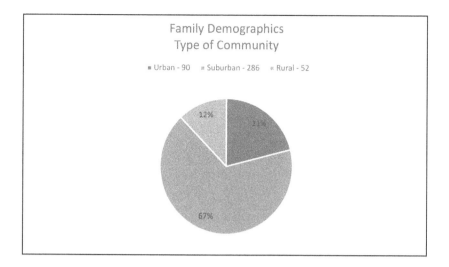

As seen in this graph, the majority of families reside in suburban areas.

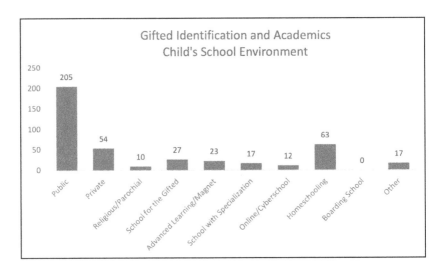

Almost half of children in this sample (47.9%) attend(ed) public school. However, more than half of the children attend(ed) other educational programs, reflecting the time and financial resources many parents expend on their gifted child's education. Interestingly, none of the children in this sample attended boarding school, which is traditionally associated with high levels of achievement. It is possible that participants who responded to this survey are not as focused on traditional values associated with achievement, and are more concerned with finding an environment suited to their child's needs. On the other hand, it is also possible that parents of children at elite boarding schools are quite satisfied with their child's education, and less likely to participate in online forums that address questions or dissatisfaction.

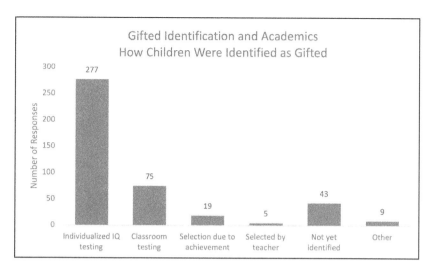

In this survey, 64.7% of children were identified through the use of individualized cognitive testing. It should be noted that many parents in the survey have young children who have not been formally tested. However, parents often qualified their assumptions about their child's suspected gifted abilities with comments about their strengths, such as precocious math or reading skills. Many school-aged children also were selected for gifted services based on more cost-effective classroom screening tools, as well as teacher selection when a child "seemed gifted" or was a high achiever. Gifted education is not legally mandated in many states or communities, so testing may not be available, and selection for enrichment or gifted services may rely on the teacher's discretion. The impetus to use local norms for identifying giftedness also may have been considered, especially in some school districts where children live in impoverished environments. This survey did not solicit information about socioeconomic status or whether families reside in locations where gifted education is mandated, so further research would be needed to clarify this. Nevertheless, individualized cognitive testing was not utilized to identify giftedness in more than one-third of the sample, so overall results may not be reflective of children clearly identified as gifted.

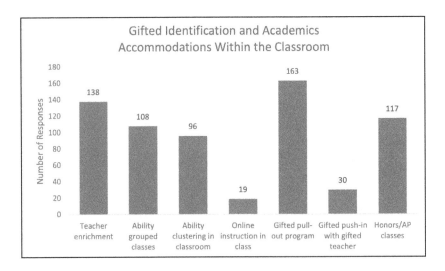

This question permitted endorsement of multiple responses. It is not surprising that the traditional gifted "pull-out" program, where students leave the classroom for a portion of the day or week, is most common. Gifted pull-out programs often provide an opportunity for creative projects or in-depth study of a particular topic of interest, along with a chance to spend time with other high ability students. However, they rarely compensate for what is missing during the remainder of the day within the regular classroom.

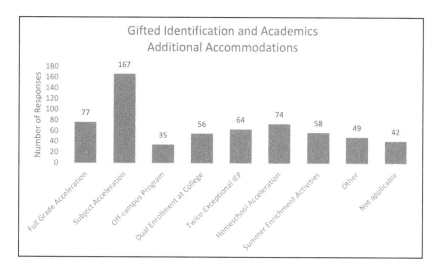

This question permitted endorsement of multiple responses. Subject acceleration was the most widely endorsed additional accommodation and is a popular and beneficial option that allows students to advance quickly in areas of strength and interest. It is least disruptive or labor-intensive for teachers and allows the child to remain with same-age peers part of the time. This option also leaves room for later off-campus or dual enrollment opportunities once the student has completed all available subject coursework offered through the school.

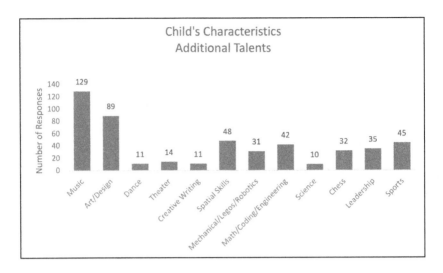

This question permitted endorsement of multiple responses. The chart above includes talents and abilities that were endorsed by at least ten participants. A variety of additional talents and abilities also were noted, including debate team, public speaking, memorization, strategic planning, proficiency with foreign languages, and additional expressions of creativity. It should be noted, though, that there were no specific criteria for what qualified as a talent or strength, and it is likely that there is wide variability in what parents may define as talent.

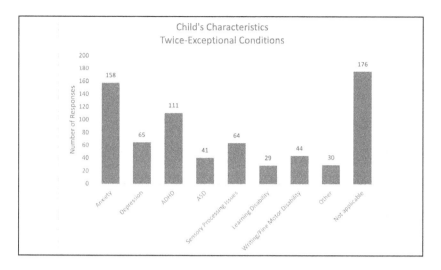

This question permitted responses to multiple items. Participants were asked to endorse any of the items listed only if their child had been diagnosed by a licensed mental health professional, physician, or specialist, such as a reading specialist or occupational therapist. The most commonly endorsed condition was anxiety (36.9%), followed by ADHD (25.9%). Fewer than half of participants (41.2%) indicated that their child does not exhibit any of the twice exceptional conditions listed in the survey

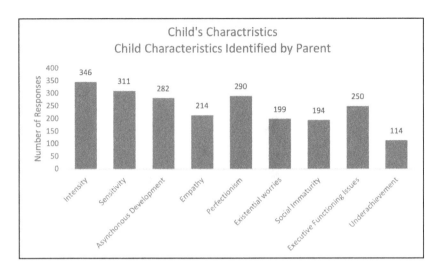

This question permitted endorsement of multiple items. Responses were based on subjective impressions from the participants, who were not asked whether these observations were supported by testing or evaluations from others. Based on parent report, intensity was observed among 80.8% of these children. Heightened sensitivity (72.6%), perfectionism (67.7%), asynchronous development (65.8%), and executive functioning issues (58.4%) also were prevalent. In fact, all items received strong endorsement from participants—even the least endorsed item, underachievement, was noted for over a quarter (26.6%) of children in this survey.

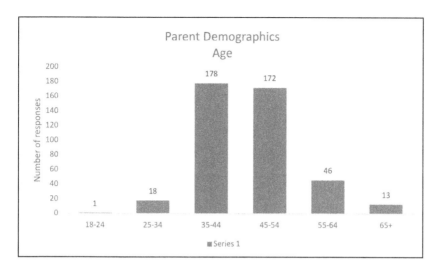

The majority of participants (81.7%) fell within the age range from 35-54. Much younger parents may not have stepped into the world of gifted advocacy yet, as their children are still young. As noted previously, "older" parents were encouraged to respond even if their child is a young adult. This would explain the number of participants who were older, along with the fact that several participants indicated that they are grandparents raising their grandchildren.

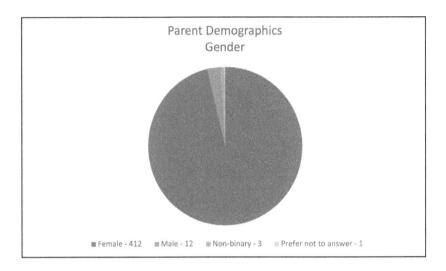

Most of the survey responses (96.2%) were completed by women. Since requests for survey participation were solicited through online and social media forums, it is not surprising that most of the responses came from women ("the moms"), who may be more comfortable communicating about their children and seeking advice online than men. However, it is possible that women are more involved in general with the "emotional work" of seeking guidance, worrying about their children, and investigating resources than men ("the dads"). More research is needed to draw any firm conclusions, though, as more responses from men likely would have been acquired if a random sample of families within the schools had been studied.

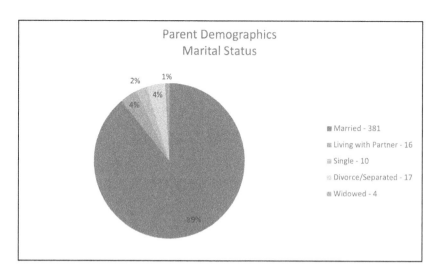

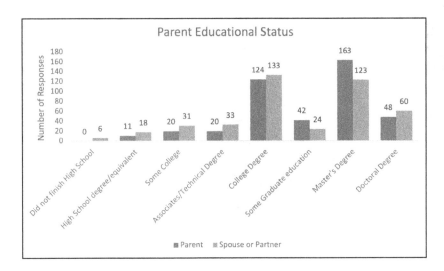

Parents in this sample are a highly educated group, with 83.7% having earned a bachelor's degree.

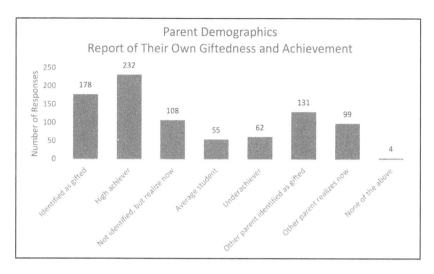

The question permitted response to multiple items. A large proportion of parents indicated that they were either formally identified as gifted or realize (now that they have a gifted child) that they are most likely gifted as well (66.8%). Many participants also indicated that the other parent of their child was either identified as gifted, or now realizes that they were most likely gifted (53.7%). More than half of participants also identified themselves as high achievers (54.2%). A much smaller percentage considered themselves average students (12.8%) or underachievers (14.4%).

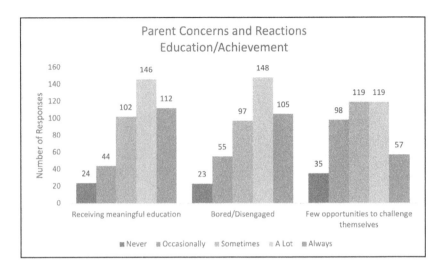

Concerns related to education were common among participants in this study, as 60.2% of parents indicated worrying a lot or always about whether their child would receive a meaningful education. Only 5.6% indicated that they never worried about this. Many also were concerned or worried about their child's level of boredom or disengagement in school (59.1%), and only 5.3% reported having no concerns about this. Many of the parents (41.1%) also reported worrying a lot or always about whether their child would find opportunities to challenge themselves in the future. It would appear that concerns about their child's level of boredom or the absence of challenging academics in the schools lead to worries that this pattern of boredom and disengagement will persist into the future.

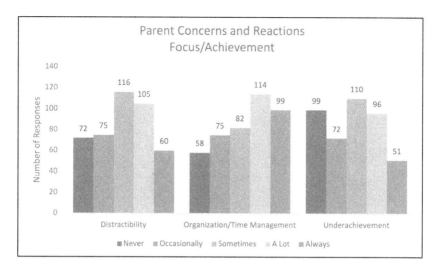

Half of the participants (49.7%) reported worrying a lot or always about their child's struggles with organization and time management. Executive functioning difficulties are prevalent among gifted children, who often experience little incentive to work hard in school. Although 38.5% of parents were concerned about distractibility, this percentage is greater than the 25.9% who indicated their child had received a diagnosis of ADHD. Despite concerns related to distractibility or executive functioning, a smaller percentage of parents (34.3%) were concerned a lot or always about their child's underachievement.

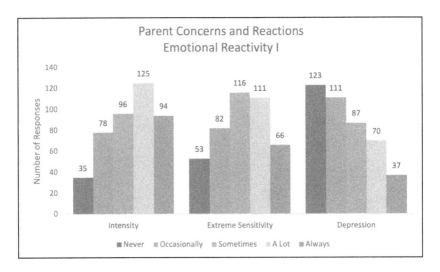

While half the parents (51.2%) indicated that they worried a lot or always about their child's intensity, and more than one-third of parents (41.3%) worried about their sensitivity. These percentages are smaller than the number who identified their child as intense (80.8%) or highly sensitive (72.6%). It is likely that while a large proportion of children in this survey were viewed by their parents as intense or highly sensitive, a much smaller percentage of parents were "worried" about the effects of these traits. A smaller percentage of parents (25%) were worried about depression. However, this number is still higher than the 15.2% of children whom parents indicated were diagnosed as depressed by a licensed mental health professional. It is possible that some gifted children in this sample struggle with a subclinical level of depression that has not necessitated an evaluation or required treatment.

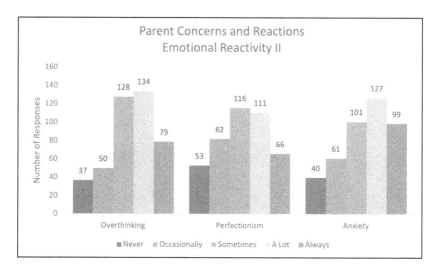

It is not surprising that many of the families worry a lot or always about their child's tendency toward overthinking (49.7%) or perfectionism (41.3%). It also is striking that many parents are worried or concerned a lot or always about their child's anxiety (52.8%), which is a much higher percentage than those who indicated that their children received a diagnosis of anxiety from a licensed mental health professional (36.9%). It is possible that some gifted children in this sample struggle with a subclinical level of anxiety that has not necessitated an evaluation or required treatment.

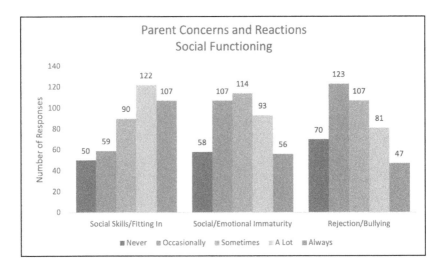

More than half of parents in this study reported feeling worried a lot or always about their child's social skills and ability to fit in with peers or find friends (53.5%). Concerns about social and emotional immaturity (34.8%) and rejection or bullying toward their child (29.9%) also were expressed.

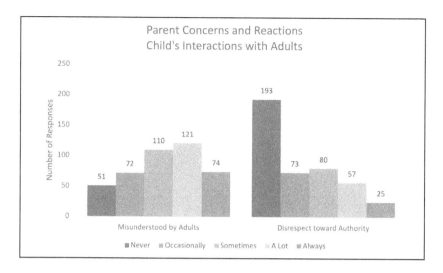

It is interesting to note that while 45.5% of parents expressed concerns that their child was misunderstood by adults a lot or always, only 19.1% were concerned that their child would show disrespect toward authority. In fact, 45% indicated that they never worried about this.

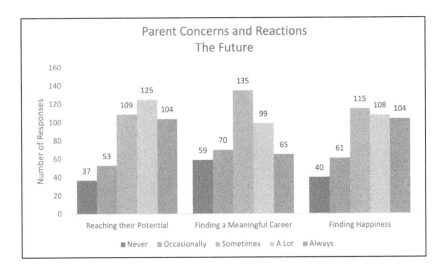

While 38.3% of parents in this study indicated worrying a lot or always about whether their child would find a meaningful career, an even higher proportion worry about whether their child will reach their potential (53.5%) or find happiness (49.5%). Clearly, many parents of gifted children actively worry not only about their child's current academic and emotional functioning, but also project fears about their well-being into the future. It is likely that some of the urgency many parents experience when advocating for their child's needs in schools rests on the assumption that without a solid foundation, they will never hit their stride, find happiness, or reach their potential.

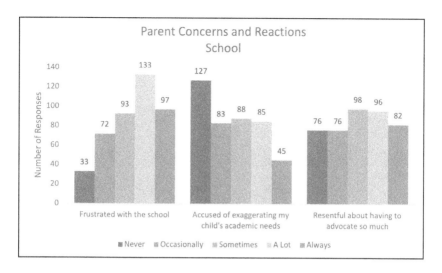

A large proportion of parents (53.7%) reported feeling frustrated a lot or always with their child's school. A sizeable number (41%) also reported resenting how much time and effort are involved with advocating for their child. Despite commonly voiced concerns about school personnel or the community at large implying that parents exaggerate their child's academic needs, a relatively small percentage of parents in this study reported feeling frustrated a lot or always about this (30.3%), and 29.6% reported never having these concerns.

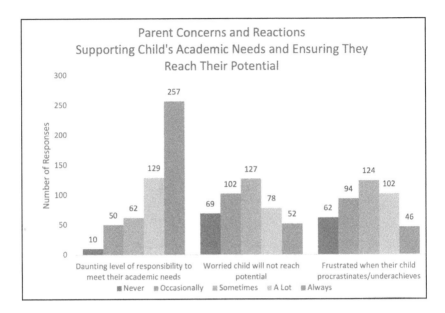

The majority of parents in this study (90%) reported feeling a daunting level of responsibility to meet their child's academic needs a lot or always. In fact, only 0.2% indicated that they never experience this concern. Despite these concerns, a smaller number are frustrated a lot or always with their child's underachievement (34.5%), or worried that their child will not reach their potential (30%).

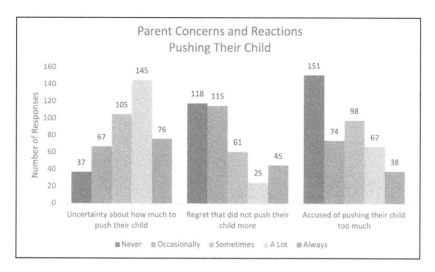

While many parents (51.6%) expressed uncertainty regarding how much they should push their child to achieve, most did not report feelings of regret for not pushing their child more, or experienced others accusing them of pushing their child too much.

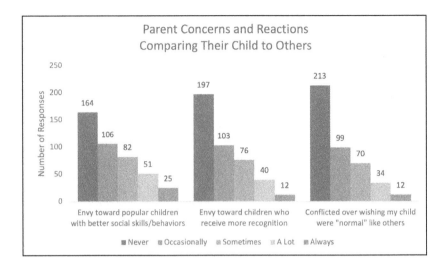

Despite commonly voiced concerns from parents of the gifted about their child's struggles, parents in this this survey did not harbor feelings of envy toward other children's achievements. Although concerned about their child's social skills or adjustment to school, it is striking that very few parents expressed feelings of envy toward other children with more polished social skills, nor did they wish their child was more like neurotypical children. In fact, 38.3% reported never feeling envy toward children with better social skills and 48.2% reported never feeling envy toward children who receive more recognition. Almost half (49.7%) reported never wishing their child were "normal" like other neurotypical children.

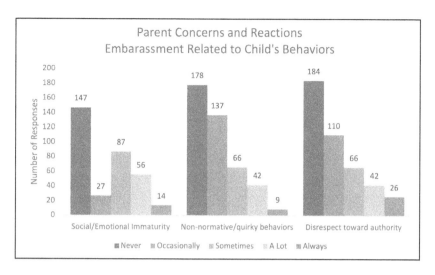

Despite commonly voiced concerns about the embarrassment parents of gifted children feel when their child disappoints, few of the parents in this study indicated that they felt embarrassed by their child's behaviors. In fact, 34.3% reported that they never feel embarrassed by their child's social or emotional immaturity, 41.5% indicated that they never feel embarrassed by quirky or non-normative behaviors, and 42.9% reported never having concerns about their child's disrespect toward authority.

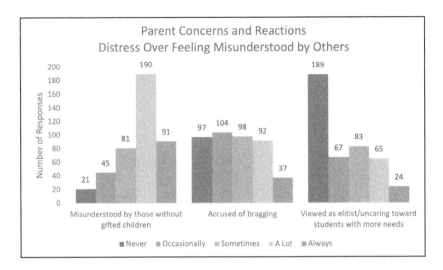

A large number of parents in this study clearly indicated that they feel misunderstood by people who do not have gifted children, with 65% indicating that they feel misunderstood a lot or always. Of interest, though, a much smaller number reported that they have been accused of bragging (30%) or viewed by others as elitist and uncaring toward students who are not gifted (20.8%). In fact, 44% indicated that they never were viewed as elitist or uncaring.

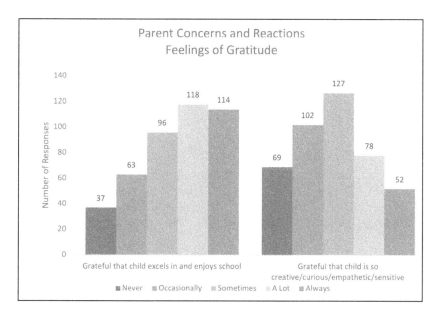

It is heartening to see how many parents in this study feel gratitude associated with the positive aspects of their child's giftedness. They appreciate their child's love of learning and heightened sensitivity, even when school environments do not always meet their needs.

End Notes

Introduction

1. Galbraith, J. & Delisle, J. (2015). *When gifted kids don't have all the answers: How to meet their social and emotional needs.* Free Spirit Publishing.

2. Post, G. (2017). Gifted underachievers under-the-radar. In R. Klingner (Ed.), *Gifted Underachiever.* Nova Science Publishers.

3. Cross, T. L. (2017). *On the social and emotional lives of gifted children. (Fifth edition).* Routledge.

4. Delisle, J. R. (2018). *Understanding your gifted child from the inside out: A guide to the social and emotional lives of gifted kids.* Routledge.

5. Inman, T. F., & Kirchner, J. (2021). *Parenting gifted children 101: An introduction to gifted kids and their needs.* Routledge.

6. Jolly, J. L., Treffinger, D. J., & Inman, T. F. (2021). *Parenting gifted children: The authoritative guide from the National Association for Gifted Children.* Routledge.

7. Neihart, M., Pfeiffer, S. I., & Cross, T. L. (2016). *The social and emotional development of gifted children: What do we know? (Second edition).* Prufrock Press.

8. Silverman, L. K. (2013). *Giftedness 101.* Springer.

9. Webb, J.T., Gore, J. L., Amend, E.R., & DeVries, A. R. (2007). *A parent's guide to gifted children.* Great Potential Press.

Chapter One

1. Silverman, L. K., & Golon, A. S. (2008). Clinical practice with gifted families. In *Handbook of giftedness in children (pp. 199-222).* Springer.

2. Reis, S. M., Baum, S. M., & Burke, E. (2014). An operational definition of twice-exceptional learners: Implications and applications. *Gifted Child Quarterly, 58,* 217-230.

3. National Association for Gifted Children. Asynchronous development. White paper. Retrieved from: https://www.nagc.org/resources-publications/resources-parents/social-emotional-issues/asynchronous-development#:~:text=Asynchrony%20is%20the%20term%20used,develop%20unevenly%20across%20skill%20levelsl

4. Terman, L. M. (2019). *The Measurement of intelligence.* Wentworth Press.

5. Warne, R. T. (2019). An evaluation (and vindication?) of Lewis Terman: What the father of gifted education can teach the 21st century. *Gifted Child Quarterly, 63,* 3–21.

6. National Association for Gifted Children, & Council of State Directors of Programs for the Gifted. (2013). *State of the states in gifted education 2012–2013: National policy and practice data.* Washington, DC: Author.

7. Callahan, C. M., Moon, T. R., & Oh, S. (2017). Describing the status of programs for the gifted: A call for action. *Journal for the Education of the Gifted, 40,* 20-49.

8. Sternberg, R. J. (2004). Introduction to definitions and conceptions of giftedness. *Definitions and conceptions of giftedness, 2,* xxiii-xxvi.

9. Goleman, D. (2005). *Emotional intelligence: Why it can matter more than IQ.* Bantam Books.

10. Gardner, H. E. (1983). *Frames of mind.* Basic Books.

11. Daniels, S., & Piechowski, M. M. (Eds.). (2009). *Living with intensity: Understanding the sensitivity, excitability, and emotional development of gifted children, adolescents, and adults.* Great Potential Press.

12. Dixson, D. D., Worrell, F. C., Olszewski-Kubilius, P., & Subotnik, R. F. (2016). Beyond perceived ability: The contribution of psychosocial factors to academic performance. *Annals of the New York Academy of Sciences, 1377,* 67-77.

13. Kaufman, J. C., Plucker, J. A., & Russell, C. M. (2012). Identifying and assessing creativity as a component of giftedness. *Journal of Psychoeducational Assessment, 30,* 60-73.

14. Lamb, K. N. (2021). Creativity. In J. A. Plucker, & C. M. Callahan (Eds.), *Critical issues and practices in gifted education (pp. 113-122).* Routledge.

15. Luria, S. R., O'Brien, R. L., & Kaufman, J. C. (2016). Creativity in gifted identification: Increasing accuracy and diversity. *Annals of the New York Academy of Sciences, 1377*, 44-52.

16. Olszewski-Kubilius, P., Subotnik, R. F., & Worrell, F. C. (2015). Antecedent and concurrent psychosocial skills that support high levels of achievement within talent domains. *High Ability Studies, 26*, 195-210.

17. Prober, P. (2016). *Your rainforest mind: A guide to the well-being of gifted adults and youth.* GHF Press.

18. Roeper, A. (1982). How the gifted cope with their emotions. *Roeper Review, 5*, 21-24.

19. Silverman, L. (2013). *Giftedness 101.* Springer Publishing Company.

20. Webb, J. T., Gore, J. L., Amend, E. R., & De Vries, A. R. (2007). *A parent's guide to gifted children.* Great Potential Press.

21. Renzulli, J. S. (2011). What makes giftedness?: Reexamining a definition. *Phi Delta Kappan, 92*, 81-88.

22. Plomin, R., & Von Stumm, S. (2018). The new genetics of intelligence. *National Review of Genetics, 19,* 148–159.

23. Papadopoulos, D. (2020). Psychological framework for gifted children's cognitive and socio-emotional development: A review of the research literature and implications. *Journal for the Education of Gifted Young Scientists, 8*, 305-323.

24. Subotnik, R. F., Olszewski Kubilius, P., & Worrell, F. C. (2011). Rethinking giftedness and gifted education: A proposed direction forward based on psychological science. *Psychological Science in the Public Interest, 12*, 3-54.

25. Silverman, L. K. (2012). *The unique inner lives of gifted children.* Pdf. http://citeseerx.ist.psu.edu/viewdoc/download?doi=10.1.1.734.1027&rep=rep1&type=pdfS

26. Columbus Group. (1991, July). *Unpublished transcript of the meeting of the Columbus Group.* Columbus, OH.

27. Brigham, F. J., & Bakken, J. P. (2014). Assessment of individuals who are gifted and talented. In J. P. Bakken, F. E. Obiakor, & A. F. Rotatori (Eds.), *Gifted education: Current perspectives and issues.* Emerald Group Publishing Limited.

28. Callahan, C. M., Renzulli, J. S., Delcourt, M. A. B., & Hertberg-Davis, H. L. (2013). Considerations for identification of gifted and talented students: An introduction to identification. In C. M. Callahan & H. L. Hertberg-Davis (Eds.), *Fundamentals of gifted education: Considering multiple perspectives (pp. 83–91).* Routledge.

29. Johnson, S. K. (2021). Definitions, models, and characteristics of gifted students. In S. K. Johnson (Ed.), *Identifying gifted students.* Prufrock Press.

30. Makel, M. C., & Johnsen, S. K. (2021). Conceptions of Giftedness. In J. A. Plucker, & C. M. Callahan (Eds.), *Critical issues and practices in gifted education.* Routledge.

31. McClain, M. C., & Pfeiffer, S. (2012). Identification of gifted students in the United States today: A look at state definitions, policies, and practices. *Journal of Applied School Psychology, 28,* 59-88.

32. National Association for Gifted Children. *Definition and rationale for gifted education.* Pdf. Retrieved from: https://www.nagc.org/sites/default/files/administrators/Rationale%20for%20Gifted%20Ed.pdf

33. National Association for Gifted Children (2019). *A definition of giftedness that guides best practice.* White paper.

34. Reis, S. M., Sullivan, E. E., & Renzulli, S. J. (2021). Characteristics of gifted learners: Varied, diverse, and complex. In F. A. Karnes, & S, M. Bean (Eds.), *Methods and materials for teaching the gifted.* Routledge.

35. Silverman, L. K. (1998). Through the lens of giftedness. *Roeper Review, 20,* 204-210.

36. National Association for Gifted Children (2019). *Key considerations in identifying and supporting gifted and talented learners: A report from the 2018 NAGC definition task force.* White paper.

37. Reis, S. M., Baum, S. M., & Burke, E. (2014). An operational definition of twice-exceptional learners: Implications and applications. *Gifted Child Quarterly, 58,* 217-230.

38. Barnard-Brak, L., Johnsen, S. K., Pond Hannig, A., & Wei, T. (2015). The incidence of potentially gifted students within a special education population. *Roeper Review, 37,* 74-83.

39. Nicpon, M. F., & Pfeiffer, S. I. (2011). High-ability students: New ways to conceptualize giftedness and provide psychological services in the schools. *Journal of Applied School Psychology, 27,* 293-305.

40. Maddocks, D. L. (2020). Cognitive and achievement characteristics of students from a national sample identified as potentially twice exceptional (gifted with a learning disability). *Gifted Child Quarterly, 64,* 3-18.

41. Ford, D. Y., Grantham, T. C., & Whiting, G. W. (2008). Another look at the achievement gap: Learning from the experiences of gifted Black students. *Urban Education, 43,* 216-239.

42. Grissom, J. A., & Redding, C. (2015). Discretion and disproportionality: Explaining the underrepresentation of high-achieving students of color in gifted programs. *Aera Open, 2*(1), 2332858415622175.

43. Henfield, M. S., Woo, H., & Bang, N. M. (2017). Gifted ethnic minority students and academic achievement: A meta-analysis. *Gifted Child Quarterly, 61,* 3-19.

44. Olszewski-Kubilius, P., & Corwith, S. (2018). Poverty, academic achievement, and giftedness: A literature review. *Gifted Child Quarterly, 62,* 37–55.

45. Card, L, & Giuliano, L. (2015). *Can universal screening increase the representation of low income and minority students in gifted education?* (NBER Working Paper No. 21519). National Bureau of Economic Research.

46. Ford, D. Y., & Grantham, T. C. (2003). Providing access for culturally diverse gifted students: From deficit to dynamic thinking. *Theory into practice, 42,* 217-225.

47. Lakin, J. M. (2016). Universal screening and the representation of historically underrepresented minority students in gifted education: Minding the gaps in Card and Giuliano's research. *Journal of Advanced Academics, 27,* 139–149.

48. Peters, S. J., Makel, M. C., & Rambo-Hernandez, K. (2021). Local norms for gifted and talented student identification: Everything you need to know. *Gifted Child Today, 44,* 93-104.

49. Plucker, J. A., Hardesty, J., & Burroughs, N. (2013). Talent on the sidelines: Excellence gaps and America's persistent talent underclass. *Center for Education Policy Analysis, University of Connecticut.* Pdf.

50. Peters, S. J., Gentry, M., Whiting, G. W., & McBee, M. T. (2019). Who gets served in gifted education? Demographic representation and a call for action. *Gifted Child Quarterly, 63,* 273–287.

51. Henfield, M. S., Washington, A. R., & Owens, D. (2010). To be or not to be gifted: The choice for a new generation. *Gifted Child Today, 33,* 17-25

52. Hartman, M. S. (2019). *The Potential Promises and Pitfalls of Using Local Norms for Gifted Identification.* West Virginia University. Pdf.

53. Peters, S. J., Rambo-Hernandez, K., Makel, M. C., Matthews, M. S., & Plucker, J. A. (2019). Effect of local norms on racial and ethnic representation in gifted education. *AERA Open, 5*(2), 2332858419848446.

54. Hamilton R, McCoach, D. B., Tutwiler, M. S., Siegle, D., Gubbins, E. J., Callahan, C. M., Broderson, A. V., & Mun, R. U. (2018). Disentangling the roles of institutional and individual poverty in the identification of gifted students. *Gifted Child Quarterly, 62,* 6-24.

55. Post, G. (2021). How to explain giftedness to your child. In A Grahl, & C. Trepanier (Eds.), *Perspectives on giftedness.* GHF Press.

56. Makel, M. C., Lee, S.-Y., Olszewski-Kubilius, P., & Putallaz, M. (2012). Changing the pond, not the fish: Following high-ability students across different educational environments. *Journal of Educational Psychology,* 104, 778–792.

57. Delisle, J., & Galbraith, M. A. (2002*). When gifted kids don't have all the answers: How to meet their social and emotional needs.* Free Spirit Publishers

58. Post, G. (2017). Gifted underachievers under-the-radar. In R. Klingner (Ed.), *Gifted Underachiever.* Nova Publishers.

59. Risemberg, R., & Zimmerman, B. J. (2010). Self-regulated learning in gifted students. *Roeper Review, 15,* 98-101.

60. Zimmerman, B. J. (2010). Becoming a self-regulated learner: An overview. *Theory into Practice, 41,* 64-70.

61. Ash, C., & Huebner, E. S. (1998). Life satisfaction reports of gifted middle-school children. *School Psychology Quarterly, 13,* 310–321.

Chapter Two

1. McDowall, J. (2019). *Exploring the experiences of New Zealand mothers raising intellectually gifted children: Maternal strains, resources, and coping behaviours.* [Master's Thesis]. University of Canterbury.

2. Roeper, A. (1982). How the gifted cope with their emotions. *Roeper review, 5,* 21-24.

3. Silverman, L. K. (2012). *The unique inner lives of gifted children*. Pdf. http://citeseerx.ist.psu.edu/viewdoc/download?doi=10.1.1. 734.1027&rep=rep1&type=pdf

4. Daniels, S., & Piechowski, M. M. (Eds.). (2009). *Living with intensity: Understanding the sensitivity, excitability, and emotional development of gifted children, adolescents, and adults.* Great Potential Press.

5. Tucker, B., & Lu Haferistein, N. (1997). Psychological intensities in young gifted children. *Gifted Child Quarterly, 41*, 66-75.

6. Webb, J. T., Gore, J. L., Amend, E. R., DeVries, A. R., & Kim, M. (2008). A parent's guide to gifted children. *Gifted and Talented International, 23*, 155-158.

7. Chang, H., & Kuo, C. (2013). Overexcitabilities: Empirical studies and application. *Learning and Individual Differences, 23*, 53-63.

8. Dabrowski, K. (1964). *Positive Disintegration.* Little Brown

9. Mendaglio, S. (2008). *Dabrowski's Theory of Positive Disintegration.* Great Potential Press.

10. Mendaglio, S., and Tillier, W. (2006). Dabrowski's theory of positive disintegration and giftedness: Overexcitability research findings. *Journal for the Education of the Gifted, 30*, 68–87.

11. Schläppy, M. L. (2019). Understanding mental health through the theory of positive disintegration: A visual aid. *Frontiers in psychology, 10*, 1291.

12. Anaïs, S. Y. (2018). *The relationship between analytical intelligence, emotional intelligence, and overexcitabilities in gifted children.* [Doctoral dissertation]. Alliant International University.

13. Wirthwein, L., & Rost, D. H. (2011). Focusing on overexcitabilities: Studies with intellectually gifted and academically talented adults. *Personality and Individual Differences, 51*, 337-342.

14. Rinn, A. N., & Reynolds, M. J. (2012). Overexcitabilities and ADHD in the gifted: An examination. *Roeper Review, 34*, 38-45.

15. DeYoung, C. G., Quilty, L. C., Peterson, J. B., & Gray, J. R. (2014). Openness to experience, intellect, and cognitive ability. *Journal of Personality Assessment, 96*, 46-52.

16. Vuyk, M. A., Krieshok, T. S., & Kerr, B. A. (2016). Openness to experience rather than overexcitabilities: Call it like it is. *Gifted Child Quarterly, 60*, 192–211.

17. McCrae, R. R., & John, O. P. (1992). An introduction to the five-factor model and its applications. *Journal of Personality, 60*, 175-215.

18. Neihart, M., & Yeo, L. S. (2018). Psychological issues unique to the gifted student. In S. I. Pfeiffer, E. Shaunessy-Dedrick, & M. Foley-Nicpon (Eds.), *APA handbook of giftedness and talent (pp. 497–510)*. American Psychological Association.

19. Szymanski, A. (2021). Social and emotional issues in gifted education. In J. A. Plucker, & C. M. Callahan, (Eds.), *Critical issues and practices in gifted education: A survey of current research on giftedness and talent development (pp. 417-430)*. Routledge.

20. Alsop, G. (1997). Coping or counselling: Families of intellectually gifted students. *Roeper Review, 20*, 28-34.

21. Silverman, L. (2013). *Giftedness 101*. Springer.

22. Tolan, S. S. (2007). *Giftedness as asynchronous development*. Retrieved from Stephanie S. Tolan Web site: http://www.stephanietolan.com/gt_as_asynch.htm

23. Webb, J. T. (2013). *Searching for meaning: Idealism, bright minds, disillusionment, and hope*. Great Potential Press.

24. Karpinski, R. I., Kolb, A. M. K., Tetreault, N. A., & Borowski, T. B. (2018). High intelligence: A risk factor for psychological and physiological overexcitabilities. *Intelligence, 66*, 8-23.

25. Webb, J. T., Amend, E. R., Webb, N., Beljan, P., Olenchak, F. R., & Goerss, J. (2005). *Misdiagnosis and dual diagnoses of gifted children and adults: ADHD, bipolar, OCD, Asperger's, depression, and other disorders*. Great Potential Press.

Chapter Three

1. Silverman, L. K., & Golon, A. S. (2008). Clinical practice with gifted families. In *Handbook of giftedness in children (pp. 199-222)*. Springer.

2. Webb, J. T. (2013). *Searching for meaning: Idealism, bright minds, disillusionment, and hope*. Great Potential Press.

3. Siegel, D. J., & Hartzell, M. (2013). *Parenting from the inside out: How a deeper self-understanding can help you raise children who thrive.* Tarcher Perigee.

4. Rimlinger, N. A. (2015). *Dwelling on the right side of the curve: An exploration of the well-being of parents of gifted children.* [Doctoral dissertation]. The Australian National University.

5. Jolly, J. L, & Matthews, M. S. (2012). A critique of the literature on parenting gifted learners. *Journal for the Education of the Gifted, 35,* 259-290.

6. National Association for Gifted Children & Council of State Directors of Programs for the Gifted (2020). *2018-2019 State of the states in gifted education (executive summary).* NAGC.org.

7. Callahan, C. M., Moon, T. R., & Oh, S. (2017). Describing the status of programs for the gifted: A call for action. *Journal for the Education of the Gifted, 40,* 20-49.

8. Colangelo, N., Assouline, S. G., & Gross, M. (2004). *A nation deceived: How schools hold back America's brightest students.* University of Iowa.

9. Delisle, J. R. (2019, November 6). Stop scapegoating gifted students for inequality. *Education Week.*

10. Moon, S. M. (2009). Myth 15: High ability students don't face problems and challenges. *Gifted Child Quarterly, 53,* 274-276.

11. Peters, S. J., Carter J., & Plucker, J. A. (2020). Rethinking how we identify "gifted" students. *Phi Delta Kappan, 102,* 8-13.

12. Steenbergen-Hu, S., Makel, M. C., & Olszewski-Kubilius, P. (2016). What one hundred years of research says about the effects of ability grouping and acceleration on K–12 students' academic achievement: Findings of two second-order meta-analyses. *Review of Educational Research, 86,* 849-899.

13. Wright, B. L., Ford, D. Y., & Young, J. L. (2017). Ignorance or indifference? Seeking excellence and equity for under-represented students of color in gifted education. *Global Education Review, 4,* 45-60.

14. Purcell, J. H., & Martinson, R. (2004). Elimination of Gifted and. *Public Policy in Gifted Education, 12,* 71.

15. Keirouz, K. (1990). Concerns of parents of gifted children: A research review. *Gifted Child Quarterly, 34,* 56-63.

16. Peterson, J. S. (2007). Myth 17: Gifted individuals do not have unique social and emotional needs. *Gifted Child Quarterly, 53,* 280-282.

17. Tolan, S. (1994). Discovering the gifted ex-child, *Roeper Review, 17,* 134-138.

18. Lewis, R. B., Kitano, M. K., & Lynch, E. W. (1992). Psychological intensities in gifted adults, *Roeper Review, 15,* 25-31.

19. Lovecky, D. V. (1986). Can you hear the flowers singing? Issues for gifted adults. *Journal of Counseling and Development, 64,* 572-575.

20. Lubinski, D., & Benbow, C. P. (2006). Study of mathematically precocious youth after 35 years: Uncovering antecedents for the development of math-science expertise. *Perspectives on Psychological Science, 1,* 316-345.

21. Park, G., Lubinski, D., & Benbow, C. P. (2007). Contrasting intellectual patterns predict creativity in the arts and sciences: Tracking intellectually precocious youth over 25 years. *Psychological Science, 18,* 948-952.

22. Prober, P. (2016). *Your rainforest mind: A guide to the well-being of gifted adults and youth.* GHF Press.

23. Rinn A. N., & Bishop J. (2015). Gifted adults: A systematic review and analysis of the literature. *Gifted Child Quarterly, 59,* 213-235.

24. Streznewski, M. K. (1999). *Gifted grownups: The mixed blessings of extraordinary potential.* Wiley.

25. Plomin, R., & Von Stumm, S. (2018). The new genetics of intelligence. *National Review of Genetics, 19,* 148–159.

26. Sauce, B., & Matzel, L. D. (2018). The paradox of intelligence: Heritability and malleability coexist in hidden gene-environment interplay. *Psychological Bulletin, 144,* 26-47.

27. Silverman, L. K., & Kearney, K. (1989). Parents of the extraordinarily gifted. *Advanced Development, 1,* 41-56.

28. Perrone, K. M., Perrone, P. A., Ksiazak, T. M., Wright, S. L., & Jackson, Z. V. (2007). Self-perception of gifts and talents among adults in a longitudinal study of academically talented high-school graduates. *Roeper Review, 29,* 259-264.

29. McDowall, J. (2019). *Exploring the experiences of New Zealand mothers raising intellectually gifted children: Maternal strains, resources, and coping behaviours.* [Master's Thesis]. University of Canterbury.

30. Colangelo, N., & Dettmann, D. F. (1983). A review of research on parents and families of gifted children. *Exceptional Children, 50*, 20–27.

31. Hackney, H. (1981). The gifted child, the family, and the school. *Gifted Child Quarterly, 25*, 51-54.

32. Fell, L., Dahlstrom, M., & Winter, D. C. (1984). Personality traits of parents of gifted children. *Psychological reports, 54*, 383-387.

33. Renati, R., Bonfilgilio, N. S., & Pfeiffer, S. (2017). Challenges raising a gifted child: Stress and resilience factors within the family. *Gifted Education International, 33*, 145–162.

34. Mathews, F. N., West, J. D., & Hosie, T. W. (1986). Understanding families of academically gifted children. *Roeper Review, 9*, 40-42.

Chapter Four

1. Matthews, M. S., Ritchotte, J. & Jolly, J. (2014). What's wrong with giftedness? Parents' perception of the gifted label. *International Studies in Sociology of Education, 24*, 372-393.

2. Rash, P.K. (1998). Meeting parents' needs. *Gifted Child Today, 21*, 14-17.

3. Silverman, L. K., & Kearney, K. (1989). Parents of the extraordinarily gifted. *Advanced development, 1*, 41-56.

4. Renati, R., Bonfiglio, N. S., & Pfeiffer, S. (2017). Challenges raising a gifted child: Stress and resilience factors within the family. *Gifted Education International, 33*, 145-162.

5. Rimlinger, N. A. (2015). *Dwelling on the right side of the curve: An exploration of the well-being of parents of gifted children.* [Doctoral dissertation]. The Australian National University.

6. Alsop, G. (1997) Coping or counseling: Families of intellectually gifted students. *Roeper Review, 20*, 28-34.

7. Greenspon, T. S. (2022). Ending the Silence of Friends: Comment on Scott Peters' "The Challenges of Achieving Equity Within Public School Gifted and Talented Programs." *Gifted Child Quarterly, 66*, 124–125.

8. National Association for Gifted Children & Council of State Directors of Programs for the Gifted (2020). *2018-2019 State of the states in gifted education, (executive summary).* NAGC.org.

9. Ditzen, B., & Heinrichs, M. (2014). Psychobiology of social support: The social dimension of stress buffering. *Restorative Neurology and Neuroscience, 32*, 149-62.

10. Leigh-Hunt, N., Bagguley, D., Bash, K., Turner, V., Turnbull, S., Valtorta, N., & Caan, W. (2017). An overview of systematic reviews on the public health consequences of social isolation and loneliness. *Public Health, 152,* 157-171.

11. Levula, A., Harré, M., & Wilson, A. (2017). Social network factors as mediators of mental health and psychological distress. *International Journal of Social Psychiatry. 63,* 235-243.

12. Lippold, M. A., Glatz, T., Fosco, G. M., & Feinberg, M. E. (2017). Parental perceived control and social support: Linkages to change in parenting behaviors during early adolescence. *Family Process, 57,* 432-437.

13. Nunes, C., Martins, C., Ayala-Nunes, L., Matos, F., Costa, E., & Gonçalves, A. (2021). Parents' perceived social support and children's psychological adjustment. *Journal of Social Work, 21,* 497–512.

14. Fouse, B, Biedelman, V., & Morrison, J. A. (1995). Keeping peace with parents of the gifted. *The Education Digest, 60,* 37.

15. Free, S. A. (2014). *Support for parents of gifted and talented children in the western region of Melbourne.* [Doctoral dissertation]. Victoria University.

16. McDowall, J. (2019). *Exploring the experiences of New Zealand mothers raising intellectually gifted children: Maternal strains, resources, and coping behaviours.* [Master's Thesis]. University of Canterbury.

17. Silverman, S. K. & Golon, A. S. (2008). Clinical Practice with gifted families. *In E. I. Pfeiffer, (ed.), Handbook of Giftedness in Children.* Springer.

18. Angley, M., Divney, A., Magriples, U., & Kershaw, T. (2015). Social support, family functioning and parenting competence in adolescent parents. *Maternal and child health journal, 19,* 67–73.

19. Armstrong, M., Lefcovitch, B., & Ungar, M. (2005). Pathways between social support, family well-being, quality of parenting, and child resilience: What we know. *Journal of Child and Family Studies, 14,* 269-281.

20. Halstead, E. J., Griffith, G. M., & Hastings, R. P. (2018). Social support, coping, and positive perceptions as potential protective factors for the well-being of mothers of children with intellectual and developmental disabilities. *International Journal of Developmental Disabilities, 64,* 288-296.

21. Leahy-Warren P., McCarthy G., & Corcoran P. (2012). First-time mothers: Social support, maternal parental self-efficacy and postnatal depression. *Journal of Clinical Nursing, 21*, 388-97.

22. Schilling, R. F., & Schinki, S. P. (1984). Personal coping and social support for parents of handicapped children. *Children of Youth Services Review, 6*, 195-206.

23. Pimentel, M. J., Viera-Santos, S., Santos, V., & Vale, M. C. (2011). Mothers of children with attention deficit/hyperactivity disorder: Relationship among parenting stress, parental practices, and behaviour. *ADHD Attention Deficit and Hyperactivity Disorder, 3*, 61-68.

24. Gerdes, A. C., & Hoza, B. (2006). Maternal attributions, affect, and parenting in attention deficit hyperactivity disorder and comparison families. *Journal of Clinical Child and Adolescent Psychology, 35*, 346-355.

25. Hayes, S. A., & Watson, S. L. (2013). The impact of parenting stress: A meta-analysis of studies comparing the experience of parenting stress in parents of children with and without autism spectrum disorder. *Journal of Autism and Developmental Disorders, 43*, 629-642.

26. Bonis, S. (2016). Stress and parents of children with autism: A review of literature. *Issues in Mental Health Nursing, 37*,153-163.

27. Cross, T. L. (2021). *On the social and emotional lives of gifted children*. Routledge.

28. Delisle, J. (2006). *Parenting gifted kids: Tips for raising happy and successful children*. Routledge.

29. Inman, T. F., & Kirchner, J. (2021). *Parenting gifted children 101: An introduction to gifted kids and their needs*. Routledge.

30. Jolly, J. L., Treffinger, D. J., & Inman, T. F. (2021). *Parenting gifted children: The authoritative guide from the National Association for Gifted Children*. Routledge.

31. Neihart, M., Reis, S. M., Robinson, M., & Moon, S. (2002). *The social and emotional development of gifted children: What do we know?* Prufrock Press.

32. Webb, J. T., Gore, J. L., & Amend, E. R. (2007). *A parent's guide to gifted children*. Great Potential Press.

33. Adler, D.A. (2006). *The effects of participating in support groups focusing on parenting gifted children*. [Doctoral dissertation]. Kent State University.

34. DeVries, A., & Webb, J. T. (2007). *Gifted parent groups: The SENG model.* Great Potential Press.

35. Dangel, H. L., & Walker, J. J. (1991) An assessment of the needs of parents of gifted students for parent education programs, *Roeper Review, 14,* 40-41.

36. Nilles, K. (2014). Parents need support, too! *Parenting for High Potential, 3*(4), 8.

37. Pearl, P. (1997). Why some parent education programs for parents of gifted children succeed and others do not? *Early Child Development and Care, 130,* 41-48.

38. Saranli, A. G., & Metin, E. N. (2014). The effects of the SENG model parent group on parents and gifted children. *Education and Science, 39,* 1-13.

39. Weber, C. L. & Stanley, L. (2012). Educating parents of gifted children: Designing effective workshops for changing parent perceptions. *Gifted Child Today, 35,* 128-136.

40. Ruf, D. L. (2021) How parental viewpoint and personality affect gifted child outcomes. *Gifted Education International, 37,* 80-106.

41. Braggett, E. J., Ashman, A., & Noble, J. (1983). The expressed needs of parents of gifted children. *Gifted Education International, 1,* 80-83.

42. Morawska, A., & Sanders., M. (2008). Parenting gifted and talented children: What are the key child behaviour and parenting issues? *Australian and New Zealand Journal of Psychiatry, 42,* 819-827.

43. Robins, J. (2011). *Starting and sustaining a parent group to support parents of gifted children.* National Association for Gifted Children.

Chapter Five

1. Chua, A. (2011). *Battle hymn of the tiger mother.* Penguin Books.

2. Bowlby, J. (1982). *Attachment and loss: Vol. I, Attachment (2nd ed.).* Basic Books.

3. Stern, D. N. (1985). *The interpersonal world of the infant. A view from psychoanalysis and developmental psychology.* Basic Books.

4. Tronick, E. (1989). Emotions and emotional communication in infants. *American Psychologist, 44,* 112-119.

5. Bruce, J., Gunnar, M. R., Pears, K. C., and Fisher, P. A. (2013). Early adverse care, stress neurobiology, and prevention science: Lessons learned. *Prevention Science, 14,* 247–256.

6. McLaughlin, K. A., Sheridan, M. A., Tibu, F., Fox, N. A., Zeanah, C. H., & Nelson, C. A. (2015). Causal effects of the early caregiving environment on development of stress response systems in children. *Proceedings of the National Academy of Sciences, 112,* 5637-5642.

7. Winnicott, D.W. (1971). *Playing and reality.* Tavistock Publications.

8. Reis, S. M., & McCoach, D. B. (2000). The underachievement of gifted students: What do we know and where do we go? *Gifted Child Quarterly, 44,* 152-170.

9. Siegle, D. (2021). *The underachieving gifted child: Recognizing, understanding, and reversing underachievement.* Routledge.

10. Post, G. (2017). Gifted underachievers under-the-radar. In R. Klingner (Ed.), *Gifted underachiever.* Nova Science Publishers.

11. Inman, T. F. (2016). What a child doesn't learn. *Parenting for high potential, 6,* 15-17.

12. Gottleib, R., Hyde, E., Immordino-Yang, M. H., & Kaufman, S. B. (2016). Cultivating the social-emotional imagination in gifted education: Insights from educational neuroscience. *Annals of the New York Academy of Sciences,* 1-10.

13. McCoach, D. B. & Siegle, D. (2003). Factors that differentiate underachieving gifted students from high-achieving gifted students. *Gifted Child Quarterly, 47,* 144-154.

14. Siegle, D., & McCoach, D. B. (2005). *Motivating gifted students.* Prufrock Press.

15. Lahey, J. (2015). *The gift of failure: How the best parents let go so their children can succeed.* Harper Collins.

16. Redding, R. E. (1989). Underachievement in the verbally gifted: Implications for pedagogy. *Psychology in the Schools, 26,* 275-291.

17. Assor, A., & Tal, K. (2012). When parents' affection depends on child's achievement: Parental conditional positive regard, self-aggrandizement, shame and coping in adolescents. *Journal of adolescence, 35,* 249-260.

18. Greenstreet, R. (2011. May 13). Lang Lang: 'I'd play the piano at 5AM.' *The Guardian.*

19. Rosin, H. (2015, December). The Silicon Valley suicides. *The Atlantic*. Retrieved from https://www.theatlantic.com/magazine/archive/2015/12/the-silicon-valley-suicides/413140/

20. Scelfo, J. (2015, July 27). Suicide on campus and the stress of perfection. *The New York Times*. Retrieved from https://www.nytimes.com/2015/08/02/education/edlife/stress-social-media-and-suicide-on-campus.html?ref=edlife&_r=0

21. Silverman, L. K. (2012). *The unique inner lives of gifted children*. Pdf. http://citeseerx.ist.psu.edu/viewdoc/download?doi=10.1.1.734.1027&rep=rep1&type=pdf.

Chapter Six

1. Silverman, L. K. (2012). *The unique inner lives of gifted children*. Pdf. http://citeseerx.ist.psu.edu/viewdoc/download?doi=10.1.1.734.1027&rep=rep1&type=pdf

2. Brown, B. (2013). *Shame vs. guilt*. Retrieved from: https://brenebrown.com/articles/2013/01/15/shame-v-guilt/

3. Myers, B. J., Mackintosh, V. H., & Goin-Kochel, R. P. (2009). "My greatest joy and my greatest heart ache:" Parents' own words on how having a child in the autism spectrum has affected their lives and their families' lives. *Research in Autism Spectrum Disorders, 3*, 670-684.

4. Woodgate, R. L., Ateah, C., & Secco, L. (2008). Living in a world of our own: The experience of parents who have a child with autism. *Qualitative Health Research, 18*, 1075-1083.

5. Eaton, K., Ohan, J. L., Stritzke, W. G., & Corrigan, P. W. (2016). Failing to meet the good parent ideal: Self-stigma in parents of children with mental health disorders. *Journal of Child and Family Studies, 25*, 3109-3123.

6. Meltzer, H., Ford, T., Goodman, R., & Vostanis, P. (2011). The burden of caring for children with emotional or conduct disorders. *International Journal of Family Medicine, 2011*, 1-8.

7. Butler, R., & Bauld, L. (2005). The parents' experience: Coping with drug use in the family. *Drugs: Education, Prevention and Policy, 12*, 35-45.

8. McDonald G, O'Brien L, & Jackson D. (2007). Guilt and shame: Experiences of parents of self-harming adolescents. *Journal of Child Health Care, 11*, 298-310.

9. Xiang, Y., Dong, X., & Zhao, J. (2020). Effects of envy on depression: The mediating roles of psychological resilience and social support. *Psychiatry Investigation, 17*, 547.

10. Burton, N. (2014). The psychology and philosophy of envy. *Psychology Today, August 21*.

11. Mujcic, R., & Oswald, A. J. (2018). Is envy harmful to a society's psychological health and wellbeing? A longitudinal study of 18,000 adults. *Social Science & Medicine, 198*, 103-111.

12. McCarthy, P. A., & Morina, N. (2020). Exploring the association of social comparison with depression and anxiety: A systematic review and meta-analysis. *Clinical Psychology & Psychotherapy, 27*, 640-671.

13. Van de Ven, N. Zeelenberg, M. & Pieters, R. (2009). Leveling up and down: The experiences of benign and malicious envy. *Emotion, 9*, 419-429.

14. Zell, A. L. (2008). Antidotes to envy: A conceptual framework. In R. Smith (Ed.), *Envy: Theory and research*. Oxford University Press.

15. Ninivaggi, F. J. (2010). *Envy theory: Perspectives on the psychology of envy*. Rowman & Littlefield Publishers.

16. Lange, J., & Crusius, J. (2015). Dispositional envy revisited: Unraveling the motivational dynamics of benign and malicious envy. *Personality and Social Psychology Bulletin, 41*, 284-294.

17. Dong, X., Xiang, Y., Zhao, J., Li, Q., Zhao, J., & Zhang, W. (2020). How mindfulness affects benign and malicious envy from the perspective of the mindfulness reperceiving model. *Scandinavian Journal of Psychology, 61*, 436–442.

Chapter Seven

1. Folkman, S., & Moskowitz, J. T. (2004). Coping: Pitfalls and promise. *Annual Review of Psychology, 55*, 745-774.

2. Segerstrom, S. C., & Smith, G. T. (2019). Personality and coping: Individual differences in responses to emotion. *Annual Review of Psychology, 70*, 651-671.

3. McDowall, J. (2019). *Exploring the experiences of New Zealand mothers raising intellectually gifted children: Maternal strains, resources, and coping behaviours*. [Master's Thesis]. University of Canterbury.

4. Free, S. A. (2014). *Support for parents of gifted and talented children in the western region of Melbourne.* [Doctoral dissertation]. Victoria University.

5. Rimlinger, N. A. (2015). *Dwelling on the right side of the curve: An exploration of the well-being of parents of gifted children.* [Doctoral dissertation]. The Australian National University.

6. Moreno-Rius, J. (2018). The cerebellum in fear and anxiety-related disorders. *Progress in Neuro-Psychopharmacology and Biological Psychiatry, 85,* 23-32.

7. DeAngelis, T. (2019, February). The legacy of trauma. *Monitor on Psychology, 50*(2). Retrieved from: http://www.apa.org/monitor/2019/02/legacy-trauma

8. Sheffler, J. L., Stanley, I., & Sachs-Ericsson, N. (2020). ACEs and mental health outcomes. In J. G. Gordon & T. O Afifi, (Eds.), *Adverse childhood experiences (pp. 47-69).* Academic Press.

9. Vig, K. D., Paluszek, M. M., & Asmundson, G. J. (2020). ACEs and physical health outcomes. In J. G. Gordon & T. O Afifi, (Eds.), *Adverse Childhood Experiences (pp. 71-90).* Academic Press.

10. Kaczkurkin, A. N., & Foa, E. B. (2015). Cognitive-behavioral therapy for anxiety disorders: An update on the empirical evidence. *Dialogues in Clinical Neuroscience, 17,* 337–346.

11. Carpenter, J. K., Andrews, L. A., Witcraft, S. M., Powers, M. B., Smits, J. A., & Hofmann, S. G. (2018). Cognitive behavioral therapy for anxiety and related disorders: A meta-analysis of randomized placebo-controlled trials. *Depression and Anxiety, 35,* 502-514.

12. Otte, C. (2011). Cognitive behavioral therapy in anxiety disorders: Current state of the evidence. *Dialogues in Clinical Neuroscience, 11,* 413-421.

13. Bandelow, B., Michaelis, S., & Wedekind, D. (2017). Treatment of anxiety disorders. *Dialogues in Clinical Neuroscience, 19,* 93–107. https://doi.org/10.31887/DCNS.2017.19.2/bbandelow

14. Greenberg, M. (2016). The psychology of regret. *Psychology Today, May 16.*

15. Connolly, T., & Zeelenberg, M. (2002). Regret in Decision Making. *Current Directions in Psychological Science, 11,* 212–216.

16. Beike, D. R., Markman, K. D., & Karadogan, F. (2009). What we regret most are lost opportunities: A theory of regret intensity. *Personality and Social Psychology Bulletin, 35,* 385-397.

17. Roese, N. J., & Summerville, A. (2005). What we regret most…and why. *Personality and Social Psychology Bulletin, 31,* 1273–1285.

18. Seltzer, L. F. (2016). How your regrets can actually help you. *Psychology Today, October 6.*

19. Bauer, I., & Wrosch, C. (2011). Making up for lost opportunities: The protective role of downward social comparisons for coping with regrets across adulthood. *Personality and Social Psychology Bulletin,* 37, 215-228.

20. Wrosch, C., Bauer, I., Miller, G. E., & Lupien, S. (2007). Regret intensity, diurnal cortisol secretion, and physical health in older individuals: Evidence for directional effects and protective factors. *Psychology and aging, 22,* 319-330.

21. Zeelenberg, M., Van Dijk, W. W., Manstead, A. S. R.,and der Pligt, J. (1998). The experience of regret and disappointment. *Cognition and Emotion, 12,* 221-230.

22. Hackney, H. (1981). The gifted child, the family, and the school. *Gifted Child Quarterly, 25,* 51-54.

23. Van Dijk, W. W., and Zeelenberg, M. (2002). What do we talk about when we talk about disappointment? Distinguishing outcome-related disappointment from person-related disappointment. *Cognition and Emotion, 16,* 787-807.

Chapter Eight

1. Winnicott, D. W. (1967). Mirror-role of mother and family in child development. *Playing and reality.*

2. Olszewski-Kubilius, P., Lee, S., & Thomson, D. (2014). Family environment and social development in gifted students. *Gifted Child Quarterly, 58,* 199-216.

. Delahooke, M. (2019). *Beyond behaviors: Using brain science and compassion to understand and solve children's behavioral challenges.* PESI Publishing

4. Nelson, J. (2006). *Positive discipline: The classic guide to helping children develop self-discipline, responsibility, cooperation, and problem-solving skills.* Ballantine Books.

5. Seay, A., Freysteinson, W. M., & McFarlane, J. (2014). Positive parenting. *Nursing Forum, 49,* 200–208.

6. Cooke, J. E., Kochendorfer, L. B., Stuart-Parrigon, K. L., Koehn, A. J., & Kerns, K. A. (2019). Parent–child attachment and children's experience and regulation of emotion: A meta-analytic review. *Emotion, 19*, 1103–1126.

7. Eisenberg, N., Zhou, Q., Spinrad, T. L., Valiente, C., Fabes, R. A., & Liew, J. (2005). Relations among positive parenting, children's effortful control, and externalizing problems: A three-wave longitudinal study. *Child development, 76*, 1055-1071.

8. Joussemet, M., Landry, R., & Koestner, R. (2008). A self-determination theory perspective on parenting. *Canadian Psychology, 49*, 194-200.

9. Smokowski, P. R., Bacallao, M. L., Cotter, K. L., and Evans, C. B. (2015). The effects of positive and negative parenting practices on adolescent mental health outcomes in a multicultural sample of rural youth. *Child Psychiatry and Human Development, 46*, 333-345.

10. Baumrind, D. (1967). Child care practices anteceding 3 patterns of preschool behavior. *Genetic Psychology Monographs, 75*, 43-88.

11. Baumrind, D. (2013). Authoritative parenting revisited: History and current status. In R. E. Larzelere, A. S. Morris, & A. W. Harrist (Eds.), *Authoritative parenting: Synthesizing nurturance and discipline for optimal child development* (pp. 11–34). American Psychological Association.

12. Dwairy, M. (2004). Parenting styles and mental health of Arab gifted adolescents. *Gifted Child Quarterly, 48,* 275-286.

13. Dornbusch, S. M., Ritter, P. L., Leiderman, P. H., Roberts, D. F., & Fraleigh, M. J. (1987). The relation of parenting style to adolescent school performance. *Child Development, 58*, 1244-1257.

14. Huey, E.L., Saylor, M.F., & Rinn, A.N. (2013). Effects of family functioning and parenting style on early entrants' academic performance and college completion. *Journal for the Education of the Gifted, 36*, 418-432.

15. Pilarinos, V. & Solomon, C. (2017). Parent styles and adjustment in gifted children. *Gifted Child Quarterly, 61,* 87-98.

16. Robinson, N.M., Lanzi, R.G., Weinberg, R. A., Ramey, S. L., & Ramey, C. T. (2002). Family factors associated with high academic competence in former Head Start children at third grade. *Gifted Child Quarterly, 46*, 278-290.

17. Cornell, D. G., & Grossberg, J. W. (1987). Family environment and personality adjustment in gifted program children. *Gifted Child Quarterly, 31*, 59-64.

18. Karnes, M. B., Shwedel, A. M., & Steinberg, D. (1984). Styles of parenting among parents of young gifted children. *Roeper Review, 6*, 232-235.

19. Siegel, D. J., & Hartzell, M. (2013). *Parenting from the inside out: How a deeper self-understanding can help you raise children who thrive.* Tarcher Perigee.

20. Kurcinka, M.S. (2006). *Raising your spirited child: A guide for parents whose child Is more intense, sensitive, perceptive, persistent, and energetic.* William Morrow.

21. Gershoff, E. T., & Grogan-Kaylor, A. (2016). Spanking and child outcomes: Old controversies and new meta-analyses. *Journal of family psychology, 30*, 453.

22. Glicksman, E. (2019). Physical discipline is harmful and ineffective. *APA Monitor on Psychology, 50 (5).*

23. Afifi, T. O., Ford, D., Gershoff, E. T., Merrick, M., Grogan-Kaylor, A., Ports, K. A., MacMillan, H. L., Holden, G. W., Taylor, C. A., Lee, S. J., & Peters Bennett, R. (2017). Spanking and adult mental health impairment: The case for the designation of spanking as an adverse childhood experience. *Child Abuse and Neglect, 71*, 24–31.

24. Durrant, J., & Ensom, R. (2012). Physical punishment of children: Lessons from 20 years of research. *CMAJ : Canadian Medical Association Journal, 184*, 1373–1377.

25. Gershoff, E. T., Lee, S. J., and Durrant, J. E. (2017). Promising intervention strategies to reduce parents' use of physical punishment. *Child abuse and neglect, 71*, 9–23.

26. Webb, J. T., Gore, J. L., & Amend, E. R. (2007). *A parent's guide to gifted children.* Great Potential Press.

27. Greene, R. (2016). *Raising human beings: Creating a collaborative partnership with your child.* Scribner.

28. Ramsburg, D. (1997). *The debate over spanking.* ERIC Digest.

29. Ginsburg, K. R., Jablow, M. M. (2020). *Building resilience in children and teens: Giving kids roots and wings.* American Academy of Pediatrics.

About the Author

Gail Post, Ph.D. is a clinical psychologist, writer, and consultant. In clinical practice for over three decades, she provides psychotherapy and parent consultations with a focus on the needs of the intellectually and musically gifted. She is also an Associate Professor of Psychiatry at the University of Pennsylvania School of Medicine.

As a parent, Dr. Post experienced the daunting task of advocating for gifted services when her children were in the schools. She co-chaired a gifted parents advocacy group, which promoted changes in how gifted children were identified and educated. After her children graduated, she continued her advocacy work through writing, consulting with parents, and offering workshops to schools and parent groups. Her long-standing blog, Gifted Challenges, was launched with the intention of furthering gifted advocacy and addressing the social and emotional challenges faced by the gifted and their families.

Dr. Post has written hundreds of blog posts and articles about giftedness for newsletter and online publications, along with several book chapters. She is passionate about advocating for the needs of gifted children, dispelling the pervasive misconceptions and stereotypes about giftedness, and supporting families in their parenting efforts. In her insightful book, *The Gifted Parenting Journey: A Guide to Self-discovery and Support*, Dr. Post combines her experience as a psychologist, parent, and advocate for change, and offers supportive tools to help parents of gifted children and teens gain greater self-awareness, confidence, and clarity. She currently lives outside of Philadelphia with her husband and several pets.

CPSIA information can be obtained
at www.ICGtesting.com
Printed in the USA
BVHW040342271022
650290BV00002B/9